All-in-One
Sunday School

Volume 1

Fall

by Lois Keffer

Group

Loveland, Colorado
group.com

Dedication

To children's workers around the world who, week in and week out,
pour themselves into loving new generations of kids into God's kingdom.

Group resources really work!

This Group resource incorporates our R.E.A.L. approach to ministry. It reinforces a growing friendship with Jesus, encourages long-term learning, and results in life transformation, because it's

Relational
Learner-to-learner interaction enhances learning and builds Christian friendships.

Experiential
What learners experience through discussion and action sticks with them up to 9 times longer than what they simply hear or read.

Applicable
The aim of Christian education is to equip learners to be both hearers and doers of God's Word.

Learner-based
Learners understand and retain more when the learning process takes into consideration how they learn best.

All-in-One Sunday School

Volume 1
Copyright © 1992, 2011 Lois Keffer

Visit our website: **group.com**

Unless otherwise indicated, all Scripture quotations are taken from the *Holy Bible*, New Living Translation, copyright © 1996, 2004. Used by permission of Tyndale House Publishers, Inc., Carol Stream, Illinois 60188. All rights reserved.

Credits
Author: Lois Keffer
Cover Design: RoseAnne Sather
Interior Design: Jan Fonda and Suzi Jensen
Illustrations: Matt Wood

ISBN 978-0-7644-4944-4
Printed in the United States of America.
16 15 14 13 12   20 19 18 17 16 15

TABLE OF CONTENTS

Introduction 5

Active Learning in Combined Classes 6

How to Get Started With *All-in-One Sunday School* 8

Quick-Grab Activities 8

THE LESSONS

1. **Caring for God's World** 10
   God Made the World; Genesis 2:15-20; Psalm 104:24
   ★ *God wants us to care for his world.*

2. **The Best Creation of All** 17
   God Creates People; Genesis 1:26-31a; Ephesians 2:10
   ★ *We are all special to God.*

3. **Promises to Keep** 24
   God Saves Noah's Family; Genesis 6:9–9:17; Isaiah 40:8
   ★ *God keeps his promises, and we should, too.*

4. **God Guides** 32
   Abraham Travels to a New Land; Genesis 12:1-7; 13:5-18, Isaiah 55:9
   ★ *God will guide us.*

5. **When Tempers Sizzle** 46
   Abraham and Lot Separate; Genesis 13:1-18; Ephesians 4:2-3
   ★ *God wants us to be peacemakers.*

6. **Can You Believe It?** 54
   The Birth of Isaac; Genesis 18:1-15; 21:1-3; Luke 18:27
   ★ *Sometimes God surprises us.*

7. **God Talk, Good Talk** 66
   Ishmael Taunts Isaac; Genesis 21:1-14; Ephesians 4:29
   ★ *God wants us to be encouragers.*

8. **When No One's Watching**. 73
Eliezer Chooses Rebekah for Isaac; Genesis 24:1-67; Matthew 25:34-40
★ *God wants us to be helpful and kind even when no one else is watching.*

9. **Circle of Forgiveness** 83
Jacob and Esau; Genesis 25–33; 1 Peter 4:8
★ *God forgives us as we forgive others.*

10. **All Kinds of Families** 92
Joseph and His Brothers; Genesis 37:1-36; Ephesians 4:29–5:1
★ *Families are important to God.*

11. **When Things Get Tough** 99
Joseph: Slave, Prisoner, Commander; Genesis 39–45; Psalm 37:3a, 5
★ *God will help us through hard times.*

12. **Happy Harvest!** 107
Giving Thanks for the Harvest; Deuteronomy 8:1-18; 26:1-2
★ *We celebrate God's goodness.*

13. **Sharing What We Have** 118
A Widow Shares With Elijah; 1 Kings 17:1-16; Philippians 4:19
★ *Because God takes care of us, we can share with others.*

INTRODUCTION

Dear friend in children's ministry,

Can you even begin to imagine how much God delights in you? With a free and joyful spirit you have chosen to give your time to nurturing his children. Not that other things don't press for your attention. But you have discerned that there is no greater calling than to model for God's kids what it looks like to live in relationship with their creator. I thank God for you!

Like you, I have always been drawn to kids, and they to me. They pick me out in grocery store lines, on busy sidewalks, and from passing cars. I think it's because they recognize someone who's never grown up! My teaching never became very "adult"—oh, no! Why? Because I saw the look of boredom that came over kids' faces when they sat down with the same ol' workbooks at Sunday school that they were used to year after year.

But when Sunday school involved active challenges, storytelling, and play, all melded into learning experiences with carefully crafted questions to help kids tie scriptural truth into their own lives—WOW! ZINGO! ZAP!—the learning lights went on! Discipline problems melted away. In our small church, grade school kids of all ages learned together.

Before we knew it, the adults wanted some of what the kids were getting, so we scheduled special intergenerational Sundays when the walls came down and the whole church learned together. And that's how the original series, *Sunday School Specials*, was born, almost 20 years ago.

At that time, we had no idea that one little book of lessons would turn into a series of four, or that the four would continue to find favor in the marketplace for years and years. Thank you to all who have faithfully bought these books! And praise God…who continues to surprise us!

So here's our new format: updated content, a fresh face, and year-long scope and sequence to turn the four *Sunday School Specials* books into *All-in-One Sunday School*. Volume 1 begins with fall quarter; Volumes 2, 3, and 4 continue with winter, spring, and summer quarters respectively. So your favorite *Sunday School Specials* lessons, plus a few totally new and updated ones, now form a through-the-year curriculum for you and your kids to enjoy together. Just so the adults don't feel left out, we've noted lessons that are appropriate for intergenerational learning.

If you have a smaller Sunday school, are cramped for space or short on teachers, *All-in-One Sunday School* is just what you need to keep lively Bible learning going in your church without stretching your resources. Best of all, you can combine your kids—and be assured that everyone will get the most out of each week's lesson to apply foundational Bible truths to their lives.

I'm so excited to make this resource available to you. I hope you'll love it as much as I've loved working on it!

Lois Keffer

ACTIVE LEARNING IN COMBINED CLASSES

Research shows people remember most of what they do but only a small percentage of what they hear—which means kids don't do their best learning sitting around a table talking! They need to be involved in lively activities that help bring home the truth of the lesson. Active learning involves teaching through experiences.

Children do things that help them understand important principles, messages, and ideas. Active learning is a discovery process that helps them internalize the truth as it unfolds. Kids don't sit and listen as a teacher tells them what to think and believe—they find out for themselves. Teachers also learn in the process!

Each active-learning experience is followed by questions that encourage kids to share their feelings about what just happened. Further discussion questions help kids interpret their feelings and decide how this truth affects their lives. The final part of each lesson challenges kids to decide what they'll do with what they've learned—how they'll apply it to their lives during the coming week.

How do kids feel about active learning? They love it! Sunday school becomes exciting, slightly unpredictable, and more relevant and life-changing than ever before. So put the table aside, gather your props, and prepare for some unique and memorable learning experiences!

Active learning works beautifully in combined classes. When the group is playing a game or acting out a Bible story, kids of all ages can participate on an equal level. You don't need to worry about reading levels and writing skills. Everyone gets a chance to make important contributions to class activities and discussions.

These simple classroom tips will help you get your combined class off to a smooth start:

♦ When kids form groups, aim for an equal balance of older and younger kids in each group. Encourage the older kids to act as coaches to help younger ones get in the swing of each activity.

♦ In "pair-share," everyone works with a partner. When it's time to report to the whole group, each person tells his or her partner's response. This simple technique teaches kids to listen and to cooperate with each other.

♦ If an activity calls for reading or writing, pair young non-readers with older kids who can lend their skills. Older kids enjoy the esteem-boost that comes with acting as a mentor, and younger kids appreciate getting special attention and broadening their skills.

♦ Don't worry too much about discussion going over the heads of younger children. They'll be stimulated by what they hear the older kids saying. You may be surprised to find some of the most insightful discussion literally coming "out of the mouths of babes."

♦ Make it a point to give everyone—not just those who are academically or athletically gifted—a chance to shine. Affirm kids for their cooperative attitudes when you see them working well together and encouraging each other.

♦ Keep in mind kids may give unexpected answers. That's okay. The answers given in parentheses after questions are simply suggestions of what kids *may* say, not the "right" answers. When kids give "wrong" answers, don't correct them. Say something like: "That's interesting. Let's look at it from another viewpoint." Then ask for ideas from other kids. If you correct their answers, most kids will soon stop offering them.

HOW TO GET STARTED WITH ALL-IN-ONE SUNDAY SCHOOL

Teaching Staff

When you combine Sunday school classes, teachers get a break! Teachers who would normally be teaching in your 4- to 12-year-old age groups may want to take turns. Or ask teachers to sign up for the Sundays they'll be available to teach.

Lessons

The lessons in the *All-in-One Sunday School* series are grouped by quarter—fall, winter, spring, and summer—but each lesson can also stand on its own. Several of the lessons contain suggestions for using an intergenerational approach—inviting parents and other adults in the congregation to join the class. You may want to schedule these lessons for special Sundays in your church calendar.

Preparation

Each week you'll need to gather the easy-to-find props in the You'll Need section and photocopy the reproducible handouts. Add to that a careful read of the lesson and Scripture passages, and you're ready to go!

QUICK-GRAB ACTIVITIES

What do you do when kids arrive 15 minutes early? When one group finishes before others do? When there's extra time after class is over? Get kids involved in a Quick-Grab Activity!

How I'm Feeling Faces Board

Use newsprint or a white board or chalk board for this activity. Write "How I'm Feeling Faces" across the top. As kids arrive, invite them to draw a face that shows how they're feeling—happy, sad, mad, rushed, excited, upset, or lonely. The first time you use this activity, explain it to the kids and brainstorm different emotions they might express on the board. Ask them to initial the faces they draw.

Encourage kids to ask questions about each other's feelings. For instance, if someone draws a sad face, a friend might say, "I'm sorry to see you drew a sad face. Did you have a bad day at school?"

This can be a great tool for kids to use to learn to care for each other in deeper, more meaningful ways. You may also want to use it during guided prayer times with the children.

By the way, don't forget to draw your own "How I'm Feeling Face." Your participation will encourage the kids to participate as well. And if they discover that you've had a rough day, you'll be surprised at how extra thoughtful they will be!

Best or Worst Thing This Week Board

You guessed it—this works just the like the How I'm Feeling Faces Board. In fact, you make want to alternate the two. Invite kids to draw or write about their best or worst experiences of the week. This board may start off with superficial experiences, but it will soon grow to a depth that surprises you.

Kids really want to tell about themselves—to know and be known. One drawback of filling every minute of Sunday school is losing that intimate moment when a child would like to talk about a concern or unburden herself of a fear. A medium such as this lets kids form a pattern of sharing themselves in a nonthreatening way, which can lead to the sense of true community we all seek within God's family.

Prep and Takedown

If kids love your class—and they will!—they'll be more than willing to do everything that needs to be done to get going. So if you need chairs, handouts or supplies arranged, task your charming youngsters with the job. Have you noticed how a child's sense of worth soars when it is his particular responsibility to see that each person has a handout? Or when she gets to pack the teacher's bag?

Small jobs like these also create ownership in the class, which translates to less discipline issues. *Hey this is my class so I'm not going to mess it up!*

Whenever you say during class, "I need a helper, " you'll get a wind-farm's worth of waving arms. The same goes for before and after class as well! So put all that youthful enthusiasm to work and you'll have kids champing at the bit before class even begins.

Jabber Mat®

Group's Jabber Mat® is an on-the-floor, all-out-fun resource loaded with games and challenges for your class. Once you've used it, you'll wonder what you ever did without it! Purchase this instant go-to activity mat from Group Publishing (group.com/jabbermat).

LESSON

1

LESSON AIM

To help kids understand that ★ God wants us to care for his world.

OBJECTIVES

Kids will

✓ play games to celebrate creation and simulate pollution;

✓ discover God's instructions about caring for the earth;

✓ evaluate ways people contribute to pollution; and

✓ plan ways to keep the earth clean and safe for living.

YOU'LL NEED

❏ 1 blindfold for every pair of kids *or* items collected from nature placed in individual lunch bags

❏ Bible

❏ newspapers

❏ paper grocery bags

❏ newsprint

❏ markers

❏ photocopies of the "God's Wonderful World" handout (p. 16)

❏ crayons

BIBLE BASIS

Genesis 2:15-20

"The Lord God placed the man in the Garden of Eden to tend and watch over it." This verse gives a solid foundation for both a work ethic and ecology, all in one sentence. God didn't leave Adam to wander aimlessly through the garden—he gave

all-in-one
SUNDAY
SCHOOL

Adam a purpose for living. Work and responsibility for our living space are not the result of human sin, but part of God's original plan for people.

God made humans the rulers and caretakers of his newly created world. It's a sacred trust that all Christians share, not only for practical reasons, but theological ones, as well.

Psalm 104:24

The great variety displayed in the natural world is a fitting tribute to the creativity of the Creator! After spending a day in nature, even the most determined agnostic must wonder how all this beauty could possibly have happened by chance.

UNDERSTANDING YOUR KIDS

This is one of many lessons in which the teachers might very well learn something from the children. Kids live in a world where the environment is often at center stage in the media. They're bombarded with messages about how to care for the earth.

It's a good thing kids are learning to "think green," because they're the ones who will live with or repair the damage done by preceding generations. Christian kids have even more reason to get involved in environmental matters. It's their God-given task!

Being excited about taking care of the environment and living out that concern on a day-to-day basis are two different matters. When you're out and about, it's sometimes easier to pitch an aluminum can in the trash than to find a recycle bin. Real conservation means remembering to turn off lights, hiking or biking instead of hitching a car ride, and cooling off in the shade instead of in the air conditioning. Kids are often tempted to do things the easy way instead of the "green" way. They need lots of encouragement and affirmation to develop and stick to an environment-conscious lifestyle that will keep God's earth green for future generations.

The Lesson 😊

ATTENTION GRABBER

Find a Tree (outdoor activity)

Tell the class you're going to begin this lesson with a very different kind of nature study. Have kids form pairs—preferably with an older and younger student in each pair. Take the group outside and walk to a place where there are several trees.

Gather everyone in the middle of the trees and say: **One partner will put on a blindfold. The other partner will lead the blindfolded partner to a tree, any tree. When you get to your tree, feel it very carefully with your hands. Try to learn everything about that tree you can without looking at it. Then your partner will lead you back to the center, spin you around three times, and take off the blindfold.**

After everyone has felt a tree, been spun around, and sat down, remove the blindfolds and find out how many kids can find the trees they touched. If it's a nice day, sit down on the grass to discuss the experience.

Ask:

♦ **What was it like to examine a tree with your hands?** (I felt silly; it felt kind of neat.)

♦ **How did you feel when you did or didn't recognized the tree you felt?** (I was glad; surprised I could recognize it.)

♦ **What do you like about trees?** (They give us shade and fruit; they're pretty to look at.)

Say: **Trees are a wonderful part of God's creation. They're part of God's gift to us, and we need to take care of them. God put trees in the garden where he made the very first man and woman. Today, we're going to talk about what happened in that garden and about the important job God gave to that first man.**

Creation Mysteries (indoor activity)

Collect several items from nature that have different textures and place them in separate brown lunch bags. You might include a smooth leaf, flower petals, a thistle, a pine branch, garden soil, a bird feather, and a rock. Have kids take turns feeling what's in each bag without looking. After everyone has had a chance to touch the mystery items, let the younger kids tell you what they think each bag contains. Then spread out the mystery items on a table.

Ask:

♦ **Which was your favorite thing to touch?** Answers will differ.

> **Teacher Tip**
>
> *If it's not possible to take your kids outside or if your area doesn't have many trees, use the Creation Mysteries Attention Grabber below.*

♦ **What can you learn about things without using your eyes?** (What they feel like; how they're put together.)

Say: **Did you know God gave us the very important job of taking care of all these things? It happened way back when God created the world. God wants us to care for his world.**
★ **Let's find out about that by taking a trip back to the beginning of the earth.**

BIBLE STUDY

The World God Made (Genesis 2:15-20)

Say: **Today we're going to make a copy of the Garden of Eden—where God put the first people he ever made.**

Have kids volunteer for the following parts by raising their hands. Explain that kids will stay in their seats now and then play their roles when you read through the Bible passage.

♦ **First of all, our garden has a man named Adam. Who wants to be Adam?**

♦ **The Bible talks about a river running through the garden. We need two or three people to stretch out on the ground to make the river.**

♦ **Now we need a couple of trees. Who wants to be a tree?**

♦ **Now we need two more trees—the tree of life and the tree of having knowledge of good and evil.**

♦ **Last of all, we need people to be all kinds of birds and animals.**

Be sure all kids who haven't been chosen for another part become birds and animals.

Say: **Great! Now we're all ready. Listen for your part and be ready to take your place in the garden as I read the story from the Bible.**

Read Genesis 2:15-20 aloud, pausing to cue kids to perform their assigned parts. Some students may be excited about this kind of Bible study and want to do it again. That's fine—do it again if you have time.

Ask:

♦ **What do you think the Garden of Eden was like?** (It was full of beautiful trees and flowers and friendly animals.)

Say: **I think Adam enjoyed living in the garden, taking care of it, and watching over all the animals. But soon Adam and Eve sinned, and God made them leave the garden. Then more and more people were born, and they began to spread all over the earth. Now we have the whole world to take care of.** ★ **God wants us to care of his world.**

Ask:

♦ **What do you think of how we're taking care of God's world?** Kids' responses will vary.

Clean Sweep

Say: **Let's see what kind of job we're doing taking care of the part of God's world we live in. We're going to go outside for a "look and listen" walk. I want you to be totally silent—no talking at all. Listen for all the sounds you can hear, and look around for any garbage or pollution you can see. Don't talk until we're sitting here in our places again.**

Take the kids for a two-minute walk. Then bring them back inside and discuss what they saw and heard. Ask about the natural sounds and the human-made sounds. Talk about natural beauty and human-made pollution. If you want, have kids go back outside and pick up any trash they saw on the walk.

Ask:

♦ **How do you think God feels when he sees how people have messed up the beautiful world he created?** (Sad; angry; disgusted.)

Say: **Let's play a game called Clean Sweep and see if that will help us understand.**

Have kids count off by threes. Have "Ones" and "Twos" form a big circle together. Give each child in the circle a sheet of newspaper. Give "Threes" each a paper grocery bag, and have them get on their hands and knees in the middle of the circle.

Say: **When I say "go," Ones and Twos will start tearing their newspapers into little pieces and throwing the pieces into the circle. The Threes will try to keep the circle clean by picking up all the paper shreds and putting them in their bags. I'll call time after one minute, and then we'll see if the Threes were able to keep the circle clean. Ready? Go!**

After the minute is up, have everyone help the Threes gather the paper shreds. Then ask:

♦ **What was this game like for you?** (It was fun, but I felt bad about making the other group work so hard.)

♦ **How is this game like what's happening in the real world?** (A lot of people are polluting and only a few are trying to clean it up; not everyone is taking care of the earth.)

♦ **How does being a Christian make a difference in the way we feel about keeping the earth clean?** (We know God made the earth so we should want to work hard to please God.)

Say: ★ **God wants us to care for his world. Tell me about the things you do to help care for the earth.** List kids' responses on newsprint.

Ask:

♦ **What else can we do to help care for the earth?** If kids haven't already mentioned these things, bring them up: We

Teacher Tip

If you have extra time, have kids return to their three groups and create posters or banners urging people to take good care of the wonderful world God has given us.

can recycle, walk or ride a bike instead of asking for a ride in a car, correctly take care of our trash, use water and other resources carefully.

Record these ideas on newsprint, as well.

COMMITMENT

Our Favorite Things

Give kids each a photocopy of the "God's Wonderful World" handout and a crayon. Point out the Bible verse at the bottom and ask a volunteer to read it aloud.

Say: **You can see this handout is divided in half. On the left side of the page, draw your favorite thing from creation—it can be a flower, a tree, an animal or even a mountain. On the right side, draw or write about one thing you'll do this week to help take care of God's wonderful world.**

Allow a few minutes for drawing and writing, and then ask volunteers to share what they drew or wrote about. Encourage kids to share their plans with their parents.

CLOSING

For All the Earth

Gather kids in a circle and lead them in sentence prayers. Have volunteers finish the sentence, "Thank you, God, for creating…" Close the prayer time by asking God's help in taking good care of his wonderful world.

GOD'S WONDERFUL WORLD

Draw your favorite thing in all of God's creation.

Draw or write about one thing you'll do this week to help care for God's world.

"O Lord, what a variety of things you have made! In wisdom you have made them all. The earth is full of your creations" Psalm 104:24.

LESSON AIM

To help kids understand that ★ we are all special to God.

OBJECTIVES

Kids will

✓ identify what makes them feel good and bad,
✓ talk about God's love for them,
✓ celebrate each other's unique characteristics, and
✓ brainstorm ways to serve God.

YOU'LL NEED

❑ balloons
❑ markers
❑ large garbage bag
❑ 9×12-inch pieces of posterboard with a small slit cut in the middle of each
❑ Bibles
❑ photocopies of the "God's Workmanship" handout (p. 23)
❑ scissors
❑ glue sticks
❑ newspapers and magazines

BIBLE BASIS

Genesis 1:26-31a

The creation of humankind is the crowning work of God's creation. Just before Adam's creation we see a unique conference between the members of the Trinity: "Let us make human beings in our image, to be like us." All people carry within them some stamp of the divine—the ability to reason, to feel emotion and become morally responsible. Six

all-in-one
SUNDAY
SCHOOL

times during the Creation story, God looked at his work and pronounced it good. After the creation of humankind, he pronounced it very good.

As teachers, we have the unique opportunity to nurture the spiritual side of children while they are spiritually open and sensitive. We can help them discover the "homing" tendency that draws them to a relationship with the God in whose image they're made.

Ephesians 2:10

God has a purpose "planned in advance" for those who choose to follow him. No one needs to feel worthless or substandard. We are God's own works of art in process!

UNDERSTANDING YOUR KIDS

It's not surprising that kids tend to value themselves as society values them. Those who are physically attractive, athletic, academically talented, or socially adept tend to feel good about themselves because they find a great deal of acceptance from others. Kids need to see the values in God's family are different. Individuals are valued as God's unique creations, no matter what the outside package looks like.

Younger kids tend to compare their abilities to others'. Those who finish last, who are the most shy, or who are the last to be picked for teams will often internalize these negative messages. "I'll never be good enough" can become a dangerous, negative mind-set very early in life.

Older kids find security through moving in flocks and through dressing, talking and acting like everyone else in their group. They need to be challenged to express their God-given individuality in creative and constructive ways.

☺ The Lesson

ATTENTION GRABBER

Balloon People

As kids arrive, give them each a blown-up balloon and a marker. Place a large garbage bag at the front of the room.

Say: **I want you to draw a portrait of yourself on your balloon. Don't let anyone else see what you're drawing. When you finish your portrait, raise your hand and I'll come and put your balloon in my garbage bag. Then we're going to try to guess which balloon belongs to which person.**

After you've gathered all the balloon-portraits, pull them from the bag one by one and have people guess who they belong to. Once kids guess whose balloon it is, give it to that person, along with a piece of posterboard. Have kids each write their name on the posterboard and then push the tied-off end of their balloon through the slit in the center of the posterboard so the balloon will stand up on its own.

Ask:

♦ **What was it like trying to draw your portrait on the balloon?** (It was hard; it made me think about what I'm really like.)

♦ **What helped you tell which balloon belonged to which person?** (The way they drew; the way it looked.)

♦ **What other things besides our appearance make us each different from everyone else?** (The things we like and don't like; the things we're good at.)

♦ **What's good about being the only person exactly like you on the whole earth?** (It makes me feel special.)

Have everyone stand in a circle holding their balloons. Then have kids each turn and face outward, take a step forward and set down their balloon.

Have kids find partners. Be sure to have older kids pair up with younger ones who are just learning to write and spell.

Say: **I want each pair to visit all the balloons in the circle. On each posterboard, write one thing about that person that makes him or her unique and special.**

Travel around to the balloons yourself and add to each posterboard. When all the pairs have visited all the balloons, have kids return to their own balloons to see what others wrote about them.

Then ask:

♦ **What was it like seeing what other people think is**

> **Teacher Tip**
>
> *Ask older kids to hold younger kids' balloons steady as they draw. Broken balloons present choking hazards; dispose of pieces promptly.*

special about you? (I was surprised; it makes me happy.)

Then say: **Today we're going to see what the Bible says about us as people and discover ★ that we are all special to God.**

BIBLE STUDY

Ups and Downs (Genesis 1:26-31a)

Have kids place their balloons along one wall of the room and then open their Bibles to Genesis 1:26-31a. Choose a narrator and three more advanced readers to read in unison the parts spoken by God. Have these four kids stand facing the rest of the class.

Before the reading, have the rest of the class suggest ways the class could act out being trees, fish, birds, livestock and creatures that crawl along the ground. Explain to the class that on your cue, they are to imitate the trees or creatures the passage tells about. Then do the reading together.

After the narrator reads the final words, "it was very good," have everyone take a bow and sit down.

Ask:

♦ **What does it mean when the verse says everything God made was very good?** (God was pleased with all parts of creation.)

♦ **What do you think about God making you very good?** (It makes me feel special; I'm surprised.)

Say: **Let's talk about what makes us feel good about ourselves and what makes us feel bad. I want everyone to sit on a chair. I'm going to read several statements out loud. If what I read would make you feel good about yourself, stand up. If it would make you feel bad, crouch down on the floor in front of your chair. If it would make you feel so-so, stay right where you are, seated on your chair.**

Read the following statements, pausing after each for kids' responses:

♦ **You forgot to brush your hair.**

♦ **You drew a really neat picture, and it was put in the school art show.**

♦ **You broke a glass in the kitchen.**

♦ **Your parents grounded you for two days for having a messy room.**

♦ **You had a fight with your brother or sister.**

♦ **You got a new outfit, and you feel really cool in it.**

♦ **You got a letter from a friend you met at camp last summer.**

♦ **You started learning a musical instrument.**

♦ **You were the first to be picked when teams were chosen.**

♦ **You realized when you got to school that you were wearing two different, unmatching shoes.**

Have kids sit down, and then ask:

♦ **Why didn't we all feel good and bad about the same things?**

♦ **What does that say about us?** (We're all different; we feel the same way about some things.)

♦ **From the list I read, which would make you feel absolutely the worst?** Allow several kids to answer.

♦ **Even if one of these things happens, why doesn't God love us less?** (God loves me no matter what.)

Say: **A lot of what makes us feel good or bad is what happens on the outside—what kind of day we're having or how we look. But God cares about who we are on the inside. He loves us because he made us, and he made us in his image.** ★ **We are all special to God.**

Ask:

♦ **What is God like?** (Great; loving; kind; just; creative.)

Say: **We are created in God's image. So we can be many of those things, too. God knows what we can be. And he wants us to become our very best for him.**

LIFE APPLICATION

God's Good Work

Give kids each a photocopy of the "God's Workmanship" handout, a pair of scissors, and a glue stick.

Have children return to the pairs they formed in the "Balloon People" activity. Point out the stack of newspapers and magazines.

Say: **I want you to work together in pairs to find the letters of your first name. Don't take more than one letter from any one place—be creative and find as many different kinds of letters as you can. Then glue the letters onto your handout to make your name.**

When all the names are complete, have kids read the verse aloud together. Say: ★ **We are all special to God...**(pointing to each child) **you, and you, and you, and you. Just as you carefully found and put together the letters of your name, God carefully put together each one of you. You are his workmanship—and we know what God makes is "very good."**

Ask:

♦ **What kinds of "good works" do you think this verse is talking about?** (It means helping people in need; telling others about Jesus; using our talents to serve God.)

COMMITMENT

Special People

Say: **We've discovered several reasons to feel good about ourselves.**

Ask:

♦ **What are they?** (God made each of us unique; God made us "very good"; he made us to do good things.)

Have kids get their balloons and form groups of about four.

Say: **Look at the things kids wrote about the people in your group. Then tell what kinds of good works each person could do for God.**

Kids might suggest things like helping parents, being kind to brothers and sisters, being honest, or being friendly to other kids.

After three or four minutes, bring everyone together.

Say: **It's exciting to think about all the possibilities in this room. You're very special, not only because of what you can do, but also because of who you are.** ★ **We're all special to God.**

CLOSING

Thanking Our Creator

Form a circle. Have kids pile all the balloons in the center of the circle. Join hands and pray: **Dear Lord, thank you for each unique person in this class. Help them each to know that on their "up" days and on their "down" days you love and care for them. In Jesus' name, amen.**

Encourage kids to take their balloons and their "God's Workmanship" handouts home and talk them over with their parents.

GOD'S WORKMANSHIP

Glue cut-out letters below to make your first name.

"GOD HaS mADE US WHat WE ArE.
iN ChrIST JESuS, God mAdE us To
dO GOod WOrKS, WHiCH GOD
PLAnNeD iN ADvaNCe FOR US TO
LIVe OUr LiVES dOiNg"
ePHESIanS 2:10

LESSON

3

LESSON AIM

To help kids understand that ★ God keeps his promises, and we should, too.

OBJECTIVES

Kids will

✓ decide whether to believe certain promises,
✓ discover how God was faithful to Noah,
✓ learn how to make promises they can keep, and
✓ discover special promises from the Bible.

YOU'LL NEED

❏ a 4×6 card
❏ scissors
❏ several oranges in a bag*
❏ wet wipes
❏ markers
❏ photocopies of the "Promise Dove" handout (p. 31)
❏ 6-inch strips of ribbon in rainbow colors
❏ cellophane tape
❏ glue sticks
❏ a hole punch (optional)
*Always check for allergies before serving snacks.

BIBLE BASIS

Genesis 6:9–9:17

If you were to ask the kids in your church to name their favorite Bible story, chances are good that the story of Noah and the ark would be among the top vote-getters. Why? There's an exciting, colorful plot, a huge "natural disaster," survivors watched over by a caring God, and a rainbow to top it all off! Even Hollywood's brightest imaginations and most fantastic special effects can't top this one.

all-in-one
SUNDAY
SCHOOL

24

What makes it even better is that "this ain't no story"! It's history, or "his-story"—God's story. It's a reliable record of what God actually did on this planet.

Despite the destruction caused by the flood, this isn't an account of vengeance—it's a story of love and promises kept. After the water recedes, God promises never again to destroy all life on earth with a flood. The rainbow seals the covenant and serves as an everlasting reminder of that promise.

But there's another significant series of promises given, acted on, and kept as the story opens. God predicts the flood, then instructs Noah to build the boat for his family and the animals. God promises that Noah and his family will enter the ark. At this point, Noah doesn't understand the full implications of this promise. But he trusts the promise maker and obeys.

Use this lesson to teach children that God keeps his promises faithfully, and we should, too.

Isaiah 40:8

In a world of confusing messages and rapid change, it's important for kids to know that they can count on God's Word. God keeps his promises today, just as he did in Noah's time.

UNDERSTANDING YOUR KIDS

What child wouldn't want to spend a few months in a floating zoo? Kids have a wonderful, God-given fascination with the diversity of God's animal creation. And that's great. But it's important not to let the natural kid-appeal of this Bible story overshadow its all-important theme: God keeps his promises.

God asked Noah to do a pretty outrageous thing. We assume that Noah's ark-building binge brought more than a few snickers from his neighbors. But God had made a covenant with Noah. A covenant is a two-way street, and Noah was determined to keep his end of the bargain.

Sometimes Christian kids who live in a secular society feel that God asks them to do some pretty hard things, too. Like returning good for evil. Walking away when test or homework answers are illicitly offered. Loving their enemies. And being faithful to their promises.

Trust, obedience, faithfulness—challenge your kids to be the Noahs of their day!

The Lesson 😊

ATTENTION GRABBER

Would Ya Believe Me?

Before class, practice cutting a 4×6 card as shown in the margin. Cutting it in this manner will allow the card to stretch over a person's head. You'll also need to hide a bag of several oranges. Fold or tie the bag shut.

As kids arrive, ask:

♦ **Would you believe me if I promised to give you a treat that's never been touched by human hands? How many would believe a promise like that?**

Invite the kids who believed you to search the room until they find the bag. Have the person who finds the bag bring it to you. Before you open it, ask:

♦ **Now how many people believe my promise that this bag contains a treat that has never been touched by human hands?** Have a child who believes you open the bag. Then toss an orange to several kids and ask them to bring the oranges to the front of the class. Help them unpeel the oranges as needed (use wet wipes to clean hands before peeling the oranges).

Ask:

♦ **Who put that snack inside that outer peeling?** (God did; the orange tree did.)

♦ **Has any person touched these orange slices before?** (No.) **Are you sure?** (Yes.)

♦ **Then did I keep my promise?** (Yes.)

Say: **Good! You ought to be able to trust the promises made by your teacher at church.**

Distribute orange slices for snacks and wet wipes for clean-up. Then choose a volunteer to come to the front of the room. Show that child your 4x6 card and ask:

♦ **Would you believe me if I promised to make this card go over your head and around your neck?** (Yes, I trust you; no, that's impossible.)

If the child doesn't respond positively, keep asking until you find someone who believes your promise. Then bring out the scissors and cut the card as shown in the margin. Slip the cut-and-stretched card over the head of the child who believed your promise. Thank your volunteer. Then ask:

♦ **When I first made these promises, how many of you believed me 100 percent? Why?** (Because we know you; because we thought there was a trick to it.)

♦ **Those of you who didn't believe me, why didn't you believe in my promise?** (Because it sounded too strange; I didn't really think you could do that.)

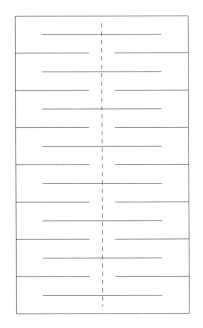

1. Fold the card in half lengthwise.
2. Cut as shown, making the first cut from the folded side, the next cut from the outside, and so on.
3. When you've made all the cuts, cut through the middle fold of all but the end strips.
4. Stretch the card open into a circle.

♦ **When you saw that I kept my first promise, did that make it easier or harder for you to believe my second promise?** (Easier, because you already did one thing that sounded hard, so I believed you could do another; harder, because it still seemed impossible to make a small card go around somebody's head.)

♦ **So when people make promises, how do you decide whether or not to believe them?** (I believe them if they've kept their promises before; it depends on their reputation.)

Say: **Today we're going to talk about the fact that ★ God keeps his promises, and we should, too.**

BIBLE STUDY

Off the Deep End (Genesis 6:9–9:17)

Say: **Our Bible story today is a pretty familiar one, so we're going to approach it differently than you've probably done before. It's about one of the most famous promises in the Bible. Does anyone care to guess what it might be?**

If no one guesses, say it has something to do with colors. If you need to give another hint, say it has something to do with colors in the sky. Then challenge kids to tell you what promise the rainbow reminds them of. If no one responds, encourage kids to listen carefully to the story to find out.

Say: **Okay, let's get started with the story of Noah. Here's what you need to do.**

Practice these cues and responses with the kids:

♦ **Whenever I say "God," fold your hands and bow.**

♦ **Whenever I say "neighbors," cover your mouth and laugh.**

♦ **Whenever I say "animals," make your favorite animal sound.**

Say: **One last thing. When I raise my hand like this** (demonstrate), **that means to cut off all noise immediately. Ready?**

Read aloud "Off the Deep End" (p. 29). Pause after each underlined word to let children respond to the cues.

Have kids give themselves a round of applause for their participation in the story. Then ask:

♦ **Why do you think Noah obeyed God and built the ark?** (Because he trusted what God said; because he wanted to make God happy.)

♦ **Why do you think Noah kept building even when his neighbors made fun of him?** (Because he trusted God more than he trusted his neighbors; because it's more important to please God than to please anyone else.)

♦ **What promises did God keep in this story?** (The promise that the flood would come; the promise to keep everyone in the ark safe; the promise never to flood the earth again.)

> ### Teacher Tip
>
> *In the middle of the story, you'll find directions to have kids form three groups and do a series of sound effects that create quite a realistic storm. The larger the group, the more effective the progressive effect as groups move from one sound to the next. If your class is small, you may want to use only two groups. Let one group do a sound effect for about five seconds before the next group joins in.*

♦ **How do you feel about people who keep their promises?** (I trust them; I respect them.)

♦ **Why is it important for Christians to keep their promises?** (So people will trust us; so people will respect our God.)

Say: **As Christians, we want to show people what God is like. When people learn that they can trust us, then someday they may learn to trust God.** ★ **God keeps his promises, and we should, too.**

LIFE APPLICATION

Pop-Up Promises

Ask:

♦ **Tell about a promise you've kept.**

♦ **Tell about a promise you made but didn't keep.**

Allow two or three children to respond to each question. Then say: **Sometimes people who don't keep their promises fail because they make promises they can't keep. I'm going to read some promises. If you think the promise I read is a good one, pop up out of your chair. If it seems like a bad promise, stay seated and point your thumbs down. Here we go.**

Pause after each promise for kids' responses.

♦ **I promise to give everyone in class a million dollars.**

♦ **I promise to try hard to be a good teacher.**

♦ **I promise that you're all going to get straight A's in school next year.**

♦ **I promise to pray for you every day this week.**

Help kids form trios. Say: **In your trios, figure out what makes a good promise and what makes a bad promise. I'll give you a minute to talk about it. Then I'll ask one person from each group to tell what you decided.**

After a minute, call time and have kids share their answers.

Then say: **Great ideas! It's important to think before you make a promise. First you think, "Is this a promise I can really keep, or do I just wish I could keep it?" Sometimes you need to ask, "Would God be happy with this promise, or am I just making this promise to get something I want?" We need to be careful about the promises we make, because** ★ **God keeps his promises, and we should, too.**

OFF THE DEEP END

One day <u>God</u> looked sadly upon the beautiful earth he'd made. Then <u>God</u> spoke to Noah. "Noah, people have ruined my beautiful earth. It's full of violence and bad things. I've decided to destroy the earth and everything in it. But I want you to build an ark for yourself and your family and two of every kind of animal. I will send a flood, and everything on the earth will die. But I promise that you and your family and the <u>animals</u> will be safe in the ark."

So Noah did just as <u>God</u> said. He began to build a boat—a huge boat—a monstrously massive and marvelous boat. The <u>neighbors</u> couldn't quite believe their eyes.

"Check out old Noah," the <u>neighbors</u> snickered. "He's really gone off the deep end now. What's he waiting for—a flood?" Then they laughed so hard they fell over. But Noah went right on building.

The next day the <u>neighbors</u> asked, "Whatcha gonna put in that incredible crate you're building?"

"<u>Animals</u>," Noah replied.

"What kinds of <u>animals</u>?" the <u>neighbors</u> asked.

"Every kind," Noah replied.

Once again the <u>neighbors</u> laughed until they fell over.

A few weeks later Noah and his family had nearly finished the ark. They started loading hay and grain and fruit inside.

"Hey!" the <u>neighbors</u> called out. "Whatcha puttin' in there now?"

"Food," Noah replied.

"For who?" the <u>neighbors</u> asked.

"For my family and the <u>animals</u>," Noah responded.

"What if the <u>animals</u> decide to eat your family?" the <u>neighbors</u> asked. They thought their question was so funny that they fell over laughing again.

When the ark was finished, <u>God</u> sent the <u>animals</u> to Noah, who began loading them in, two by two. The <u>neighbors</u> had never seen anything quite like this. They laughed a little bit...then scratched their heads.

When little raindrops started to fall, Noah's family went into the ark, and <u>God</u> shut the door. The <u>neighbors</u> looked at the ark all loaded and closed up. And they looked at the dark clouds rolling across the sky. Then the rain came harder and faster, so they ran for shelter. They weren't laughing anymore.

Let's make our own rainstorm to see what it was like when the water rose and covered the whole earth. We'll start by forming three groups. (Indicate where "Ones," "Twos" and "Threes" will be divided.) When I look at your group, start doing what I'm doing. Keep doing the same thing until I look at your group and change the action.

(Look at the Ones and rub your hands together. Then proceed to the Twos, and finally to the Threes. Come back to the Ones and snap your fingers quickly. After a few seconds give the same cue to the Twos, then to the Threes.

Continue in this manner. The third cue is patting your legs lightly, and the fourth is stomping your feet. Have the storm decrease by working backward through the cues. Have groups return to patting their legs, then snapping their fingers, then rubbing their hands together. Finally, cut the groups off one by one by raising your hand.)

Finally the rain stopped. All the people and <u>animals</u> in the ark were safe and well. Then one day the ark bumped into the top of a mountain. The water was starting to go down.

Noah sent a raven and then a dove out of the ark. But the dove came back because there was no place to land. A week later Noah sent the dove out again. This time it came back with a leaf in its mouth. Seven days later Noah sent the dove out again. This time it didn't come back, for it had found a place to nest.

Then <u>God</u> told Noah to come out of the ark. So out came Noah and his family and all the <u>animals</u>. Noah built an altar to thank <u>God</u> for keeping his promise. Then <u>God</u> blessed Noah and his family and all the <u>animals</u>. And <u>God</u> hung a shining rainbow in the sky as a promise never to destroy the world with a flood again.

29

COMMITMENT

Promise Doves

Say: **Let's make reminders of the promise God made to Noah.** Have kids form pairs, matching older kids with younger, nonreading kids. Distribute scissors, markers, and photocopies of the "Promise Dove" handout. Ask a volunteer to read aloud Isaiah 40:8 from the handout.

Ask:

♦ **What does this promise from the Bible mean to you?** (That God keeps his promises; that God's Word is true.)

Say: **That verse is God's promise to you. On the blank side of your dove, write a promise you'd like to make to God. When you've finished writing, cut out the dove.**

If children have trouble thinking of promises they'd like to make to God, suggest ideas such as "I promise to pray every day," "I promise to give God first place in my life," or "I promise to do my best to be like Jesus."

As kids are working, distribute several 6-inch strips of ribbon in rainbow colors to each child. Demonstrate how to position the strips of ribbon inside the dove; then tape the ribbons in place. Have kids rub glue sticks along the other edge of the doves and then press the two halves of the doves together.

Teacher Tip

If you have extra time, you may punch a hole in the top of each dove and tie a strip of ribbon through the hole as a hanger.

CLOSING

Promise Prayers

Have kids stand in a circle holding their promise doves. Go around the circle and invite kids to share the promises they wrote to God.

Then close with a prayer similar to this one: **Thank you, Lord, for keeping your promises. Help us trust you the way Noah did. And help us make wise promises and keep them. In Jesus' name, amen.**

Encourage kids to hang their promise doves in a special place as a reminder that ★ God keeps his promises, and we should, too.

PROMISE DOVE

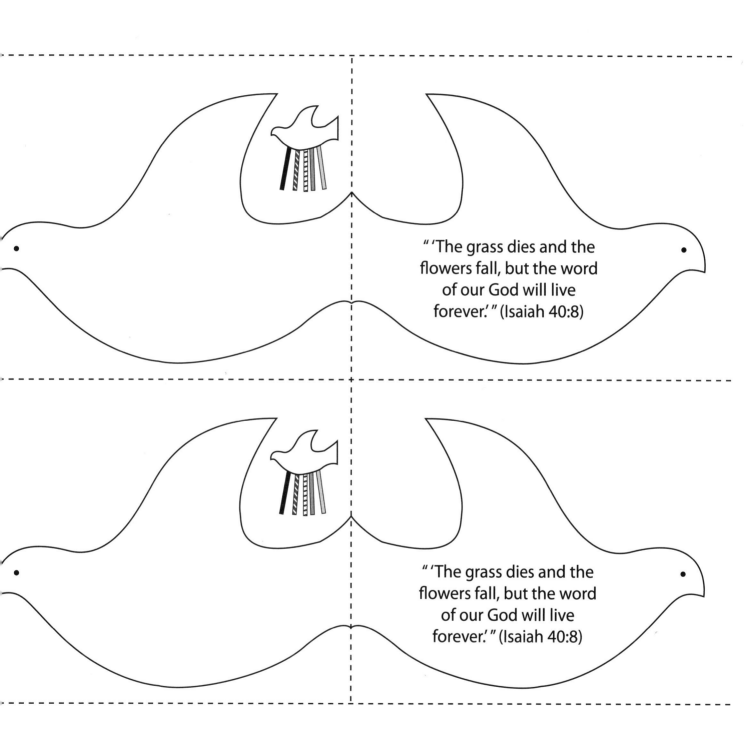

" 'The grass dies and the flowers fall, but the word of our God will live forever.' " (Isaiah 40:8)

" 'The grass dies and the flowers fall, but the word of our God will live forever.' " (Isaiah 40:8)

LESSON

4

LESSON AIM

To help kids understand that ★ God will guide us.

OBJECTIVES

Kids will

✓ search for a treat with the help of a guide who can't talk,
✓ hear how God guided Abraham,
✓ discover how to tune in to God's guidance, and
✓ make a commitment to follow God's guidance.

YOU'LL NEED

❏ a Bible
❏ Hershey's Kisses chocolates*
❏ photocopies of Figures 1, 2, and 3 (pp. 41-43)
❏ gray, red, and tan construction paper
❏ scissors
❏ a 100-piece puzzle
❏ lunch bags
❏ razor knife
❏ photocopies of the "Life's Road Map" handout (p. 44)
❏ photocopies of the "God's Road Signs" handout (p. 45)
❏ paper
❏ markers
*Always check for allergies before serving snacks.

BIBLE BASIS

Genesis 12:1-7; 13:5-18

Abraham spent the first part of his life in the cities of Ur and Haran, centers of commerce, culture, and worship of the moon god. Ruins of the famous ziggurat of Ur, a shrine to the moon god, can still be seen today. Somehow, in the midst of

all-in-one
SUNDAY
SCHOOL

these cultural distractions, God got Abraham's attention and called him to leave his familiar surroundings and set out for an unknown destination in the wilderness of Canaan.

To his credit, Abraham wasted no time. At the age of 75, he gathered his family, possessions, herds, flocks, and servants and set out to follow the living God. All God told Abraham of his destination was that it was "the land I will show you" (Genesis 12:1). God attached a promise to his directions: He would make of Abraham's family a great nation through which all the people of the world would be blessed. Setting out in blind faith, Abraham followed God, his unseen guide. His willingness to hear and obey God resulted in the birth of two great nations and, ultimately, the Savior of the world, Jesus Christ.

Isaiah 55:9

At times even the most mature Christians struggle to understand what God is doing in their lives. Who hasn't looked toward heaven in frustration and asked, "Lord, how can this be part of your plan for me?" We would like God to submit a blueprint for our lives so that we could approve it or ask for revisions! God seldom shows us the whole picture but asks instead that we trust his supreme wisdom and love for us.

UNDERSTANDING YOUR KIDS

The cultural distractions Abraham faced pale in comparison to what kids face today. From the moment they wake in the morning until they click off their stereos at night, kids are bombarded with sophisticated messages from a culture that wants to convince them that material possessions and self-gratification bring happiness. In the midst of this media melee, how can kids learn to hear the quiet voice of God?

Typically our attention turns to God when we face a crisis. Natural disasters, financial problems, the serious illness of a loved one—all these things can call our attention away from the busyness of life and cause us to take a long look at our priorities and values. But it's even harder for children to think of how daily events impact their lives as a whole. Use this lesson to teach kids that life is a series of choices and that when they choose to stop and listen to God, God will always guide them toward the right choices.

The Lesson 😊

ATTENTION GRABBER

Finders, Eaters

Help kids find partners, pairing older children with younger ones. Have each pair decide which person will leave the room and which person will stay. Say to the kids who are leaving: **You'll be the "finders." I'd like you to step out of the room for just a moment.**

Give each of the remaining partners two Hershey's Kisses chocolates. Say: **You'll be the "guides." These chocolates are for you and your partner. Hide the two of them together somewhere in this room.** Give kids a few moments to hide their candy. When the candy is hidden, have the children line up facing you.

Say: **When your partners come back into the room, your job is to guide them to the candy you've hidden. But you may not use words, and you may not move your feet or your legs. Ready?**

Call in the finders and say to them: **While you were out of the room, your partner hid a treat for the two of you. Your partner's job is to guide you to that treat without using any words and without moving his or her feet. Your job is to pay close attention to your partner and see if you can figure out where he or she is trying to guide you. If you find the treat, bring it back to your partner and enjoy it together. Ready? Go!**

Allow a couple of minutes for partners to work together. Kids who don't know what to do may pick up on other pairs' tactics. Stop the game before anyone becomes too frustrated. Let guides retrieve any treats that haven't been found yet and share the treats with their partners.

When all the kids have their treats, clap your hands to bring everyone together. Ask:

◆ **Those of you who found your treats, what did your guides do to show you the way?** (Used hand signals; nodded his head; she pointed.)

◆ **Guides, what was it like not to be able to use words or move your feet?** (Frustrating; fun and challenging.)

◆ **What was it like if you weren't able to find your treats.** (I got a little worried; I couldn't figure out how other people found theirs.)

◆ **Tell about a time when you had a hard time finding your way somewhere?** (Once I had a hard time finding the way to my piano teacher's house; once I couldn't find my parents at the mall.)

◆ **Tell about a time you followed a guide—in a museum**

or on a hike or canoe trip, for instance. (We had a guide who took us on a nature hike at a state park; a guide showed us around an art museum.)

♦ **What's good about having a guide?** (Guides know a lot about places, so you learn a lot; with a guide you don't have to worry about getting lost.)

Say: **Today we're going to learn that ★ God will guide us. Our Bible story is about a man who took his whole family into the wilderness, following a guide he couldn't even see. Do you think you'd do that? Let's find out more about this brave man and his very special guide.**

BIBLE STUDY

Abraham's Journey (Genesis 12:1-7; 13:5-18)

Before class copy Figure 1, the ziggurat, onto gray paper. Copy Figure 2, the altar, onto red paper. Copy Figure 3, the town and the wilderness, onto tan paper.

Open your Bible to Genesis 12 and explain that today's Bible story comes from Genesis, the first book of the Bible.

Fold the gray construction paper in half horizontally, along the dotted line.

Say: **Abraham lived in a big city called Ur. The people of Ur were very rich, and Ur was full of beautiful things. The most famous building in Ur was a ziggurat** (ZIG-oo-rat). **Can you say that with me? Ziggurat. Let me show you what the ziggurat looked like.**

Cut from A to B.

It was tall and wide and had lots of stairs going right up to the very top.

Open the center fold; then fold back on Line C so Figure 1 can stand by itself.

People went up the stairs to worship the moon god. That made God very sad. But Abraham wasn't like all the other people in Ur. Abraham worshipped the true God. He knew it was silly to worship the moon. Abraham knew that our God made the moon, the stars, and the whole beautiful world we live in.

One day God said to Abraham, "Leave this country and go to a new land that I will show you." Ask:

♦ **Do you think God gave Abraham a map? Why or why not?** (No, because God doesn't do things that way; no, Abraham could probably get a map somewhere else.)

♦ **Do you think God put up road signs in the wilderness? Why or why not?** (No, God probably decided just to tell Abraham where to go.)

♦ **How do you think Abraham felt about taking off into**

Teacher Tip

Kids will be fascinated with the figures you fold and cut as you tell the Bible story. Practice folding and cutting each figure ahead of time so you'll feel confident as you present the story to them.

the wilderness without knowing where he would end up? (He might have been a little scared, but he wouldn't have gone unless he trusted God.)

Say: **Abraham did exactly as God said. He packed up all his things on camels and said goodbye to the beautiful city of Ur.**

Set Figure 1 aside.

Abraham's family traveled hundreds and hundreds of miles to the new land where God wanted them to live. Ask:

♦ **How many of you have moved to a new place?**

♦ **Did you know where your new house was?** Let students respond.

♦ **What would it be like to move without knowing where you'd end up?** (Really scary; kind of weird.)

Say: **Week after week they traveled through the hot desert. Every day Abraham trusted God to show him where to go. Finally Abraham and his family arrived in the land of Canaan. God spoke to Abraham again and said, "I will give this land to you and to your children." Abraham was glad to be in the new land God had promised to show him.**

Fold the red construction paper vertically along the dotted line and cut from A to B.

Abraham was glad to be far away from the ziggurat where people worshipped the moon. In Abraham's new land, everyone would worship God.

Cut from B to D. Then open the center fold and fold back on Line C. Hold up Figure 2 with the fire folded back, out of sight.

Abraham took big stones and built an altar to God. Then Abraham built a fire on the altar and worshipped God.

Fold forward on Line C so the fire appears.

When Abraham traveled to the land of Canaan, he took everything he owned. Abraham was very rich! He had lots of tents, lots of silver, lots of gold, and herds and herds of animals.

Abraham's nephew Lot traveled with Abraham. Lot was rich, too. So with all of Abraham's sheep and Lot's sheep, there wasn't enough grass and water to go around, and their servants started to fight.

Pick up the tan construction paper.

The fighting made Abraham sad. He knew that God didn't lead him to a new land to start a fight. So he called Lot and said, "Our people shouldn't be fighting. Just look around."

Fold the tan construction paper in half on Line A.

"There's plenty of land here for everyone. So you choose where you want to go. Then I'll go the other way." Because Abraham was older, he could have said, "I'm the head of the family, so I'll pick first." But Abraham trusted God to guide

him, so he let Lot pick first.

Cut from B to C.

Lot looked to the east. Guess what he saw.

Unfold the paper; then fold back on Line D so just the city shows.

He saw a beautiful valley with a city.

Refold on the center line and turn the paper over.

Then Lot looked to the west.

Cut from E to F. Then unfold the paper and fold back on Line G so just the wilderness is showing.

Lot saw a wilderness with rugged hills, not too much water, and no cities. What do you think Lot chose?

Turn the paper so the city is showing.

Lot chose the beautiful valley with the city. But that didn't bother Abraham at all. Abraham knew God would guide him, so he was happy to live in the wilderness. God did guide Abraham, and he became the father of many nations. Thousands of years later, Jesus was born from Abraham's family.

★ God will guide us just as he guided Abraham. And when we follow God, great things can happen in our lives.

(Adapted from *Clip & Tell Bible Stories,* copyright © 1995 Lois Keffer. Published by Group Publishing, Inc., 1515 Cascade Ave., Loveland, CO 80538.)

LIFE APPLICATION

Pieces of the Puzzle

Purchase a jigsaw puzzle of not more than 100 pieces. Or glue a medium-sized poster to a sheet of poster board and then cut it into puzzle pieces. This activity works best with a fairly complex picture rather than a large, simple image. Before class, separate the puzzle pieces into four piles. Put each pile of pieces in a lunch bag.

Say: **Abraham trusted God completely, even when it meant leaving his home and traveling hundreds of miles in the wilderness. Let's have some fun finding out why we can trust God just as Abraham did.**

Help kids form four groups. The groups don't have to be exactly the same size, but it's helpful to have a similar number of older and younger children in each group. Hand a bag of puzzle pieces to each group and designate separate areas of the room where groups can work.

Say: **In your bag you'll find a puzzle. I'll give you a couple of minutes to put your puzzle together. As soon as you're absolutely sure you know what's pictured on your puzzle, raise your hands. I'll come to your group so that you can**

Teacher Tip

If you have more than 20 children, use two puzzles and have four groups work on each puzzle.

whisper it to me.

Give groups a minute or two to work on their puzzles. Since each group has just a portion of the puzzle, it's unlikely that any group will be able to guess what the finished picture will be. Before kids get frustrated, call everyone together and ask:

♦ **Why haven't you been able to figure out your puzzle?** (Some pieces must be missing.)

Say: **Then it looks like we'll have to get all the groups together to complete the puzzle. I'd like each group to choose one representative to bring your puzzle pieces and work on finishing the puzzle.**

Indicate a table or open floor space in the middle of the room where the four representatives can put the puzzle together. Invite the rest of the kids to stand behind and offer help and encouragement. When the puzzle is finally completed, have a big round of applause. Then gather everyone in a circle and ask:

♦ **Why did everyone have to work together to figure out what picture was on this puzzle?** (Because we all had parts of it; because no group had enough pieces.)

Say: **That's kind of the way life is. We just see little pieces of the picture, a day at a time. We don't know what our lives will be like a year from now or even a day from now. But God does. Listen to what God says in Isaiah 55:9: "Just as the heavens are higher than the earth, so my ways are higher than your ways and my thoughts higher than your thoughts."**

Ask:

♦ **What does that verse mean to you?** (That God knows more than we do; that God can see everything, and we can see only a little.)

Say: **God has given us good minds, but we can see and understand only a little. On the other hand, God sees and knows everything about us. And on top of that, God loves us very much. That's why we—like Abraham—can trust that ★ God will guide us. God sees the whole picture and wants to guide us in ways that are best for us. That means we need to trust God, even when we don't know exactly how things are going to turn out. Now let's look at some different ways to tune in to God's guidance.**

COMMITMENT

Life's Road Map

Make enough photocopies of the "Life's Road Map" handouts for each person to have one. Before class, use a razor knife or rotary cutter to open the dashed-lined slits marked on the handouts. You'll also need one photocopy of the "God's Road Signs" handout for every two people. Cut the road signs apart and sort them into four piles. Write the numbers 1 through 4 on four separate sheets of paper and place them at four different locations in the room. Set all the copies of Road Sign 1 by the number 1, all the copies of Road Sign 2 by the number 2, and so on.

Give everyone a copy of the "Life's Road Map" handout. Have kids count off by fours. Send the Ones to Road Sign 1, the Twos to Road Sign 2, the Threes to Road Sign 3, and the Fours to Road Sign 4.

When kids have gathered by the appropriate road signs, say: **Choose a reader and a discussion leader for your group. The reader will read your road sign aloud. Then you'll all fold your road signs and push them through the slits marked on your "Life's Road Map" handouts. When your road signs are in place, the discussion leader will ask: "How can we do what these verses teach us?" After a few minutes, I'll clap my hands, and everyone will rotate clockwise to the next road sign.**

Circulate among groups to answer questions and offer ideas and encouragement. After two or three minutes of discussion, clap your hands and have groups rotate. Repeat the process two more times so each group collects and discusses all four road signs. Then clap your hands to bring everyone together. Ask:

♦ **How can we be sure that ★ God will guide us?** (Because God guided Abraham; because the Bible tells us that God will guide us.)

♦ **What did you learn about how to tune in to God's guidance?** (We need to pray; we should study the Bible; Christian teachers can help us; we need to decide to follow God.)

Say: **Those are all good things, and they will all help you discover God's guidance. Right now, turn to a partner and tell him or her what you'll do this week to follow God.**

Allow a few moments for partners to share.

CLOSING

On Our Way

Say: **I hope you'll keep your road map and review what the Bible verses teach you to do. When we do our best to follow God, we can be sure that ★ God will guide us. When you go home, share your road map with your family and tell them what you learned about how God guides us.**

Here's a fun song that will help you remember the things we learned today. Lead children in singing this song to the tune of "Yankee Doodle."

> **God will guide us every day**
> **And show us what to do.**
> **Just as God led Abraham,**
> **God will guide us, too.**
>
> **Decide that you will follow God;**
> **Read the Bible carefully.**
> **Pray and listen every day**
> **And learn from what your teachers say.**

Close with a prayer similar to this one: **Dear God, thank you for guiding Abraham. Please guide us and help us follow you this week. In Jesus' name, amen.**

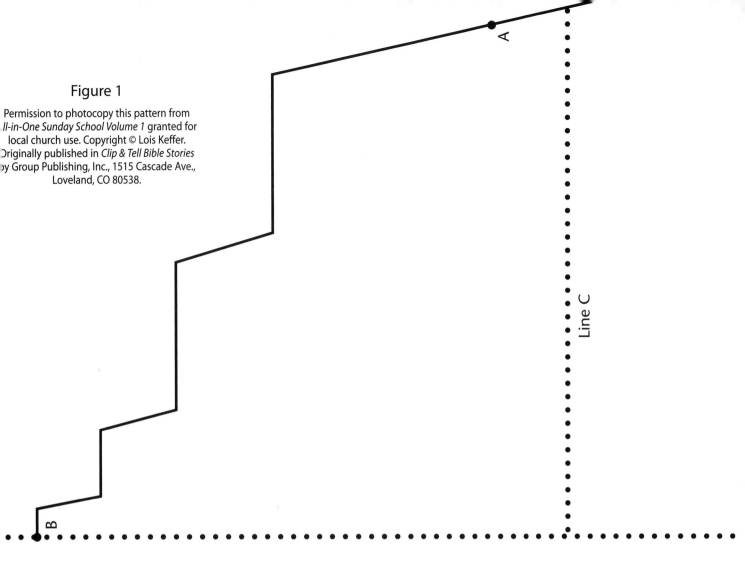

Figure 1

A

B

Line C

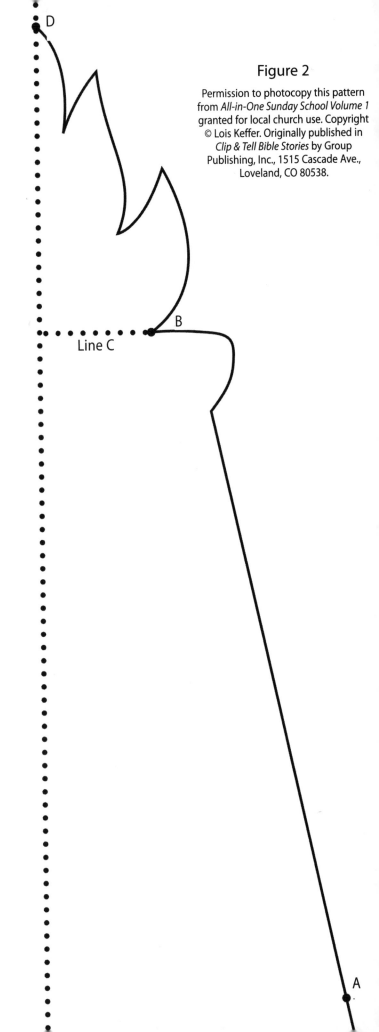

Figure 2

Line C

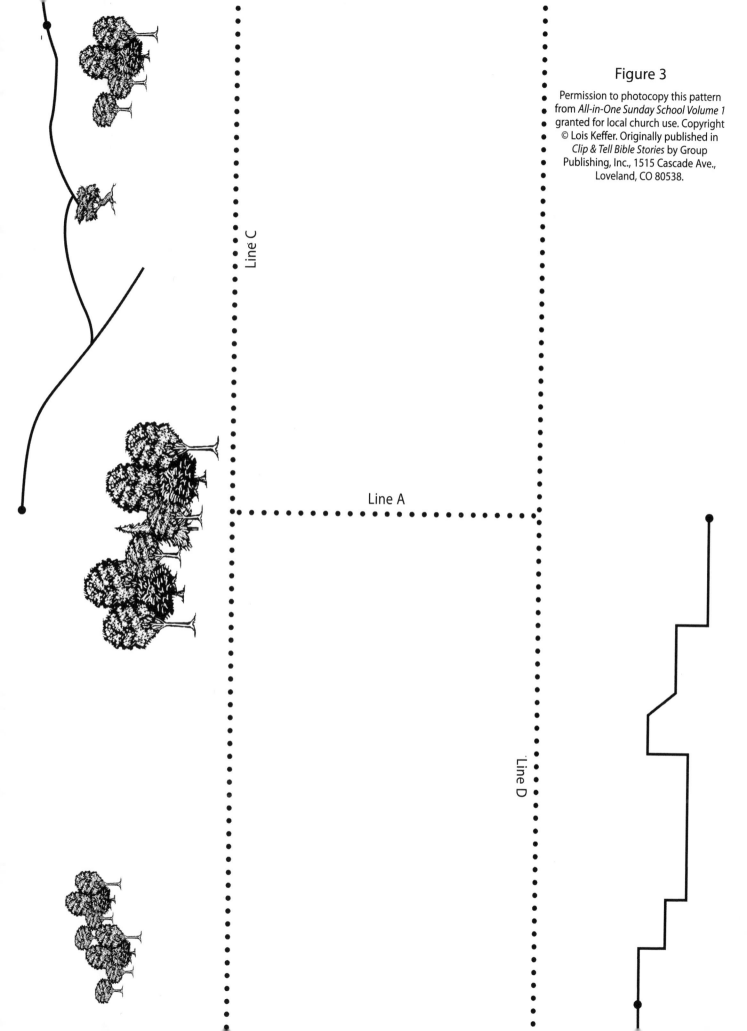

Line C

Line A

Line D

Road Sign 4

Road Sign 3

Road Sign 2

Road Sign 1

Life's Road Map

God will guide us.

GOD'S ROAD SIGNS

1. DECIDE TO FOLLOW GOD.
"Trust the Lord with all your heart; do not depend on your own understanding. Seek his will in all you do, and he will show you which path to take" (Proverbs 3:5-6).

2. READ GOD'S WORD.
"Your word is a lamp to guide my feet and a light for my path" (Psalm 119:105).

3. PRAY AND LISTEN TO GOD EVERY DAY.
"If you go the wrong way—to the right or to the left—you will hear a voice behind you saying, 'This is the right way. You should go this way' " (Isaiah 30:21, NIV).

4. LEARN FROM CHRISTIAN TEACHERS.
"Listen to the words of the wise" (Proverbs 22:17a).

"Jesus said to all of them, 'If people want to follow me, they must give up the things they want. They must be willing to give up their lives daily to follow me' " (Luke 9:23, NIV).

"All Scripture is given by God and is useful for teaching, . . . for teaching how to live right" (2 Timothy 3:16, NIV).

"When the Spirit of truth comes, he will lead you into all truth" (John 16:13a).

"Let the teaching of Christ live in you richly. Use all wisdom to teach and instruct each other by singing psalms, hymns, and spiritual songs with thankfulness in your hearts to God" (Colossians 3:16, NIV).

1. DECIDE TO FOLLOW GOD.
"Trust the Lord with all your heart; do not depend on your own understanding. Seek his will in all you do, and he will show you which path to take" (Proverbs 3:5-6).

2. READ GOD'S WORD.
"Your word is a lamp to guide my feet and a light for my path" (Psalm 119:105).

3. PRAY AND LISTEN TO GOD EVERY DAY.
"If you go the wrong way—to the right or to the left—you will hear a voice behind you saying, 'This is the right way. You should go this way' " (Isaiah 30:21, NIV).

4. LEARN FROM CHRISTIAN TEACHERS.
"Listen to the words of the wise" (Proverbs 22:17a).

"Jesus said to all of them, 'If people want to follow me, they must give up the things they want. They must be willing to give up their lives daily to follow me' " (Luke 9:23, NIV).

"All Scripture is given by God and is useful for teaching, . . . for teaching how to live right" (2 Timothy 3:16, NIV).

"When the Spirit of truth comes, he will lead you into all truth" (John 16:13a).

"Let the teaching of Christ live in you richly. Use all wisdom to teach and instruct each other by singing psalms, hymns, and spiritual songs with thankfulness in your hearts to God" (Colossians 3:16, NIV).

LESSON AIM

To help kids learn that ★ God wants us to be peacemakers.

OBJECTIVES

Kids will

✓ discover how venting anger can hurt people,
✓ learn how Abraham unselfishly settled a conflict,
✓ apply new techniques for settling conflicts, and
✓ make a commitment to express anger appropriately.

YOU'LL NEED

❏ a can of soft drink*
❏ newsprint
❏ markers
❏ masking tape
❏ 2 bags of large marshmallows*
❏ photocopies of the "Peacemaker Certificate" handout (p. 53)
❏ pencils
*Always check for allergies before serving snacks.

BIBLE BASIS

Genesis 13:1-18

Abraham and Lot had traveled together from Egypt and were preparing to set up more permanent residence in Canaan. As the patriarch, Abraham had every right to tell Lot where to go and when to leave. Instead, he chose to avoid conflict and allowed Lot to take the fertile land in the valley. What a contrast to the "fight for your rights" mentality we see so often in today's society!

Abraham was able to surrender his rights because he trusted God completely. God honored that trust by promising Abraham the whole land and a nation of descendants to fill it.

all-in-one
SUNDAY
SCHOOL

Ephesians 4:2-3

Humility, gentleness, patience, and love are not always the easiest qualities to demonstrate, especially when a person is unjustly jailed! But Paul lived what he taught, and he challenged believers—then and now—to strive for those characteristics, as well.

UNDERSTANDING YOUR KIDS

A lot of Christian kids grow up thinking it's wrong to get angry. But the truth is, anger is a healthy human emotion. Depending on the cause of the anger, there's often nothing wrong with getting angry. But there is something wrong with expressing our anger in ways that hurt people—including ourselves. Interestingly enough, it also appears to be just as harmful in the long run to try to stifle and deny anger as it is to vent it in rage.

Younger kids will often burst into tears and stomp their feet when conflict gives way to anger. Kids in the primary years may resort to hitting and name-calling. Older elementary kids may use sarcasm and mockery to vent their feelings.

Kids of all ages can learn simple techniques to help bring their feelings under control and work toward a solution. Slammed doors and name-calling don't make for positive change. An honest, open discussion of the source of conflict does.

The Lesson 😊

ATTENTION GRABBER

Caution: Explosives!

Take kids outside to an open, grassy area or a parking lot and form a circle. Toss a can of soft drink up in the air and catch it yourself. As you catch the can, finish the sentence: "It really makes me mad when . . ." Then toss the can to someone across the circle. Have that person finish the same sentence and then toss the can to another person. If you have lots of small children, you might want to have kids just hand the can to them.

Keep going until everyone in the circle has caught the can and told what makes him or her mad. If the can gets dropped and well shaken up in the process, so much the better. If the can hits the ground and pops open before you finish, skip to the second question below.

Have the last person toss the can back to you. Shake it a little and ask:

♦ **What's going to happen when I open this can?** (It's going to explode; it'll make a big mess.)

Go ahead and open the can, being careful to aim the spray away from yourself and toward the empty center of the circle. Kids will probably scream in delight as the soft drink blasts from the container.

Ask:

♦ **Why did the can blow up like this?** (Because we tossed it around.)

♦ **How is this like what happens when people get angry?** (They get so mad they blow up and yell at everyone around them.)

♦ **When have you ever gotten angry and blown up like this?** Allow several kids to reply.

♦ **Does blowing your top make things better? Why or why not?** (Not usually, it just makes others mad at me; yes, I feel better.)

Say: **It never really pays to blow your top. It's a lot smarter to learn how to handle conflicts and arguments so things get better—not worse.** ★ **God wants us to be peacemakers. Today's Bible story is about a man who knew how to do that. Let's see what we can learn from him.**

BIBLE STUDY

Keeping the Peace (Genesis 13:1-18)

Lead children inside.

Say: **First we have to set up the scene for this story. Let's form two groups. Count off by twos.**

The Ones are over here—you're Abraham's group. The Twos stand on this side of the room. You're Lot's group.

Ask for a volunteer from each group—one to play the role of Abraham, and the other to play the role of Lot. Have the two volunteers stand face to face, with their feet planted and their arms crossed.

Say: **The Bible says both Abraham and Lot were very wealthy. They had lots of money and flocks and herds and tents. Let's have two people from each group put their hands together over their heads in an arch to make a tent.**

Now I need some people to be the flocks—drop down on all fours and say "baa." Have all but two or three kids remaining in each group be the sheep.

Then say: **Good! Now these flocks need some shepherds. So the rest of you are shepherds. Pretend you have a staff in one hand.**

Now listen and do your part as I tell the story. The tents will move when I say so, the sheep will "baa" when I mention sheep, the shepherds will do what I say in the story, and Abraham and Lot will act out their parts and move their lips when they're supposed to be talking. Listen carefully for when you're supposed to move and what you're supposed to do. Is everybody ready?

Read the story "Abraham and Lot" on the next page, pausing to allow kids to do their actions.

Have all your kids give themselves a round of applause. Then ask:

♦ **Why didn't Abraham fight for his rights?** (He didn't want a fight; he cared more about keeping the peace than getting the good land.)

♦ **What happened to Abraham because he acted unselfishly?** (God blessed him and promised to give him the whole land.)

♦ **What was more important to Abraham than getting his own way?** (Keeping the peace.)

♦ **What advice do you think Abraham would give us about settling arguments?** (Think about the other person's feelings; don't always insist on your rights; be willing to compromise.)

List kids' responses on newsprint taped to the wall.

Then say: **Those are all really good ideas. And they work, too. But when there's a problem, we don't always think about the other guy's feelings. We think about our rights**

ABRAHAM AND LOT

God told Abraham and his nephew Lot to move from Egypt to the land of Canaan. Abraham and Lot were both very wealthy men, so they had to move their tents and their sheep and their shepherds. When they got to the place called Bethel, Abraham bowed down and worshipped the Lord.

But soon a problem arose. Abraham and Lot had so many sheep there wasn't enough grass and water to go around. The sheep got very thirsty. Abraham's shepherds and Lot's shepherds started fighting.

"Our master is greater than your master, so move your sheep," Abraham's shepherds said.

"But we got here first, so go find water somewhere else," Lot's shepherds argued.

Meanwhile, the poor sheep got thirstier and thirstier. Abraham and Lot were sitting in their tents when they heard about their shepherds fighting. They both shook their heads and then went out to talk things over.

Abraham said: "Let's not quarrel about this. After all, we're family. Look over this whole land and choose the part where you want to live. If you go one way, I'll go the other."

Abraham really didn't have to be so nice. Because he was older, he was the boss and could have chosen first. But Abraham trusted God to work things out, so he let Lot make the first choice.

Lot looked to the right and to the left. On one side was a valley with lots of grass and water and even some cities. On the other side stood rugged mountains and wilderness.

Lot said: "I'll take the plain. You take the mountains."

So Lot moved his tents and his sheep and his shepherds toward the city in the valley. Abraham moved his tents and his sheep and his shepherds toward the mountains.

Abraham kept the peace, even though it meant living in rougher territory. God blessed Abraham and promised to give him the whole land. Lot, who chose selfishly, got in big trouble moving to the wicked city and barely escaped with his life!

and what we want and how we feel and BOOM!—suddenly we're in the middle of a big fight.

LIFE APPLICATION

Marshmallow Madness

Say: **Let's have a big fight right now—just to see what it feels like.**

Have kids help you lay a masking tape line down the middle of the room. Have Abraham's group form a team on one side of the line, and Lot's group form a team on the other. Give each team a bag of large marshmallows.

Say: **Okay, you guys are really mad at each other—so mad you're ready to throw marshmallows! So go ahead and explode. Throw all the marshmallows you can at the other team. When you get hit by a marshmallow, throw it right back at the other team. When I call time, the team with the most marshmallows on its side loses. Ready? Go!**

Call time after about two minutes. Count up the marshmallows on each side and declare the winners and losers.

Then ask:

♦ **How does it feel to be a winner?** (Great!)

♦ **How does it feel to be a loser?** (Awful.)

♦ **How was this marshmallow war like a real argument?** (We fought as hard as we could; we tried to hurt them more than they hurt us; it got kind of out of control.)

♦ **How was it different from a real argument?** (Nobody really got hurt; we're not really mad at each other; everyone is still friends.)

♦ **How could we have made this come out with no winners or losers?** Kids may or may not realize that if no one had thrown any marshmallows, both teams would have had the same number, and no one would have won or lost.

Say: **It's fun throwing marshmallows back and forth. But it's not fun when we let our anger explode and start exchanging hurtful words. ★ God wants us to be peacemakers, even if it means giving up some of our rights as Abraham did.**

> ### Teacher Tip
>
> *If you'd rather not use marshmallows for this activity, you could try soft foam balls or wadded-up newspapers. You might want to have your older kids throw underhand and be gentle toward smaller kids. Even marshmallows can sting if they're thrown hard enough.*

COMMITMENT

Pointers for Peace

Give kids each a photocopy of the "Peacemaker Certificate" handout and a pencil. Ask a volunteer to read the Bible passage aloud. Then have kids take turns reading the peacemaking pointers in the corners. Discuss how each one can help kids control their anger and start working toward a peaceful solution.

Then have volunteers role play as many of the following situations as you have time for. Do each role-play twice. The first time, have kids get angry and shout. The second time, have the kids use the advice on the certificate to work toward a peaceful resolution.

Here are the situations:

♦ **Your brother borrowed your bicycle. The next day you go to ride it and discover it has a flat tire.**

♦ **Someone accidentally runs into you in the hall at school and knocks your books all over the floor.**

♦ **You didn't hang up your clothes, and your mom is really angry with you.**

♦ **Your sister is playing loud music and it's driving you crazy.**

♦ **Your younger brother knocked over and destroyed your latest creation using LEGO toys.**

After the role-plays, say:

These peacemaking ideas really work! They worked for Abraham, and they can work for you. ★ God wants us to be peacemakers. If you're ready to work at being a peacemaker, sign your name on your certificate.

CLOSING

People at Peace

Gather kids in a circle and have them put their arms around each other's shoulders. Close with prayer, asking God to help kids work for peace and trust the outcome to him.

As kids leave, encourage them to share the peacemaking ideas on their certificates with their families.

Peacemaker Certificate

Think about how the other person feels.

_____

is an official peacemaker.

(name)

"Always be humble and gentle. Be patient with each other, making allowance for each other's faults because of your love. Make every effort to keep yourselves united in the Spirit, binding yourselves together with peace" Ephesians 4:2-3.

Stop and count to 10.

Think of ways to compromise.

Trust God for the results.

Can You Believe it?

LESSON AIM

To help kids understand that ★ sometimes God surprises us.

OBJECTIVES

Kids will

- ✓ succeed at a seemingly impossible feat,
- ✓ hear Sarah tell how God surprised her,
- ✓ be challenged to trust God to do the impossible, and
- ✓ commit to looking for God's surprises.

YOU'LL NEED

- ❑ a paper sack of small prizes or treats*
- ❑ a bowl of raw potatoes*
- ❑ plastic drinking straws
- ❑ Bibles
- ❑ an adult to play the role of elderly Sarah (optional)
- ❑ a photocopy of the "God's Good Surprises" handout (p. 64)
- ❑ photocopies of the "Surprise Pop-Up" handout (p. 65)
- ❑ markers
- ❑ glitter glue
- ❑ scissors
- ❑ tape

* Always check for food allergies before serving snacks.

BIBLE BASIS

Genesis 18:1-15; 21:1-3

Among fascinating Bible heroines, Sarah certainly holds her own. Think about her life. She willingly followed Abraham from the culturally advanced city of Ur to an unknown destination in a wilderness hundreds of miles away. She went along with Abraham's cowardly schemes to pass her off as his sister so he wouldn't be killed for his beautiful wife. When she

proved to be barren, she urged Abraham to have a child by her servant girl. Sarah certainly can't be faulted for lack of courage! Having been barren during her childbearing years, Sarah must have given up all hope of having Abraham's son. When she was old enough to be a great-great-grandmother, three strangers appeared near Abraham's tents. The Bible text suggests that at least two of the visitors were angels, and the third is referred to as "the Lord" (18:1). When the Lord stated that Sarah would have a child before the year was out, Sarah laughed audibly. But she didn't have the last laugh, for despite Sarah's doubts, Isaac made his appearance as predicted.

Luke 18:27

The concept of "impossible" doesn't lie within God's modus operandi. You'll find it all in the Bible—from speaking the world into existence, parting the sea, and making the sun stand still to raising people from the dead. God can do the impossible today just as he did centuries ago.

UNDERSTANDING YOUR KIDS

It's a sad fact of life that kids need to be skeptics by the time they're ready to start school. "Don't talk to strangers." "Don't believe everything you hear on TV." "Walk away from anyone who tries to give you money or candy." "Don't listen to most of what's on the radio." Kids and parents know that a certain amount of skepticism is healthy and necessary.

Here's the good news: We don't have to urge kids to be skeptics when it comes to believing in God. The Bible is true—always. God keeps his promises—always. God can do anything—period. Ain't it great? Use this lesson to teach children to expect the unexpected from our incredible God.

The Lesson 😊

ATTENTION GRABBER

Do the Impossible

You'll need a small prize for each child, such as a pack of sugarless gum or a coupon for an ice-cream cone. Hide the prizes in a paper sack and set the sack out of sight.

Set out a bowl of raw potatoes and a stack of plastic drinking straws. You'll need one potato and one straw for each child. You may want to scrub the potatoes so kids don't soil their clothes.

As kids arrive, give them each a potato and a straw.

Say: **I have a great prize for anyone who can poke a straw clear through a potato. No fair using a knife or breaking your potato. I'll give you a minute or two to see if you can accomplish this amazing feat. Remember, there's a prize to be won, so give it your best shot!**

Give kids a couple of minutes to try to get their straws through their potatoes. If anyone succeeds, tell him or her not to let anyone else know how to do it. If no one succeeds, have children set their straws and potatoes aside.

Say: **I guess I'll just have to keep the prizes for myself. Or I could let you in on the secret of how to do this trick.** Let the kids egg you on. Then say: **Oh, all right. I guess since I'm such an amazingly wonderful teacher, I'll show you how to do it. But before I do, I need to know something.** Ask:

♦ **Do you believe I can poke a straw through this potato? Why or why not?** (No, because if we couldn't do it, you can't either; no, because a straw isn't strong enough to go through a potato; yes, because you've read about how to do it.)

Say: **Stand up if you think I can poke this straw through this potato. Okay, now I'll need a drumroll from everyone who's standing. Pat your hands on your legs while your truly amazing teacher performs this truly amazing feat.**

Cover the top of the straw with your thumb and poke it through the potato in one firm stroke.

Then say: **Wow! That really is amazing, isn't it? I guess since I'm the only one who did it, I should keep the prizes for myself. No? Okay, here's how you do it: Cover the top of the straw with your thumb and hold it there tightly as you punch the straw through.**

Help each child accomplish the trick, and then pass out the prizes. Have children set their potatoes, straws, and prizes by one wall of the room. Explain that they can take these things home after class and show the trick to their families. Ask:

Teacher Tip

It's actually quite easy to poke a straw through a potato. Simply cover one end of the straw with your thumb. The pressure created by the trapped air keeps the walls of the straw rigid. Practice this trick before class so you can perform it confidently in front of the kids.

56

♦ **Do you think this is an amazing trick? Explain.** (Yes, because a straw doesn't seem strong enough to go through a potato; no, because the air inside the straw helped it go through.)

♦ **Were you surprised when you were able to push your straw through your potato? Why or why not?** (Yes, because it sounds impossible; no, because I saw you do it.)

Say: **Well, the truth is, I'm not so amazing. The directions for doing this are in our lesson for today. Anyone could read the book and learn to do the trick. But I know someone who *is* truly amazing – Jesus!**

Our story today is about our truly amazing God and how he did something that surprised everyone. In fact, what God did was much more surprising than poking a straw through a potato. We're going to hear the story from a very old woman named Sarah. Sarah found out that ★ sometimes God surprises us. I want you to treat Sarah like a respected guest when she comes to our class.

BIBLE STUDY

Sarah's Surprise (Genesis 18:1-15; 21:1-3)

Say: **Sarah lived a life full of adventure. She and her husband, Abraham, left their life in the city and traveled hundreds of miles to the land of Canaan, where God wanted them to live. God promised Abraham that he would be the father of many nations and that there would be as many members of his family as there are stars in the sky.**

But there was just one problem. Years and years went by, and Sarah never had a baby. Finally Abraham and Sarah were old enough to be great-great-grandparents, but they still didn't have a child. Sarah must have given up hope. But she found out that ★ sometimes God surprises us. Let's hear the rest of the story from Sarah herself. Look! Here she comes now!

Have "Sarah" say: **Thank you for inviting me to your class today. I want to tell you about the biggest surprise of my life. You can help me tell my story by watching me carefully and doing the same actions I do.**

Have Sarah read the poem "Sarah's Surprise" (pp. 62-63) and then wave goodbye as the kids give her a round of applause. Then ask:

♦ **Why did Sarah laugh when she heard one of the visitors say she would have a baby in a year?** (Because she was too old to have a baby; because she had given up on having a baby.)

Say: **The Bible tells us that the three visitors Sarah talked about were not ordinary people. They may have been angels. The Bible even calls one of them the Lord.** Ask:

> ### Teacher Tip
>
> *You may want to invite an older woman or someone from your congregation who's a good actor to visit your class in Bible costume to read the poem. Or simply drape a shawl around your head and shoulders and read the poem yourself.*
>
> *Hint: Kids really enjoy hearing a male teacher read in a quavery, grandmotherly voice.*

♦ **Why do you suppose God waited so long to give Abraham and Sarah a baby?** (So they would know it was a special baby; so only God could make it happen.)

Say: ★ Sometimes God surprises us. God doesn't run on clocks and calendars as we do. God has all the time in the universe. Abraham and Sarah worried about getting older and not having a baby, but they were thinking about "people time," not God's time.

Let's take a few minutes to think about how God might surprise people today.

LIFE APPLICATION

Angels in Africa

Say: In the 1950s, God surprised some people in the country of Kenya. Listen carefully and see if you can tell how God surprised the people in this story.

Missionary children from all over Africa attend the boarding school at Kijabe mission station in the beautiful country of Kenya. Kijabe is one of the largest mission stations in the world.

One night all those years ago, the missionaries at Kijabe noticed a huge fire at a neighboring village not more than two miles away. Orange and yellow flames licked at the night sky, signaling danger. A friend from the burning village ran to the mission station with the terrifying news that the rebel Mau Mau tribe had attacked and burned the village, and they were coming to Kijabe next!

The missionaries gathered to pray. They had only a barbed wire fence and one policeman to protect themselves and the missionary children from the attacking Mau Maus.

Pause at this point and ask:

♦ **How do you think God will surprise the people in this story?** Let several children guess; then continue with the story.

The missionaries prayed all night. As dawn broke quietly over the Kenyan countryside, the residents of Kijabe could hardly believe they hadn't been attacked. No one knew why the Mau Maus didn't attack that night. The story finally came out when some of the rebels were captured.

"We planned to attack Kijabe," the Mau Maus confessed, "but when we got close, guardians blocked our way."

The police were still bewildered. There were no soldiers at Kijabe that night. And besides, the Mau Maus wouldn't have been afraid to fight soldiers.

"The guardians we saw were giant, flaming figures,"

Teacher Tip

You may want to choose a mature, confident reader to read this story. Sometimes hearing a different voice helps kids who are growing restless refocus on the lesson.

58

the Mau Maus explained. "We were terrified, and we all ran away!"

Ask:

♦ **Who did God surprise in this story?** (The missionaries and the Mau Maus.)

♦ **How did God surprise the Mau Maus?** (By sending flaming guardians to block the road and protect the mission station at Kijabe.)

♦ **How did God surprise the missionaries?** (God kept them from being attacked when they knew attackers were on their way.)

♦ **What do you think the giant, flaming figures were?** (Angels; helpers from God.)

♦ **If you had been at Kijabe that night, what would you have learned?** (That God is powerful; that we don't know what God will do; that God can surprise us.)

Distribute Bibles and say: **Let's see what the Bible says about what God can do.** Have children look up Luke 18:27. Encourage readers to share their Bibles with nonreaders. Ask a volunteer to read the verse aloud. Then ask:

♦ **What does this verse teach us about God?** (That God can do anything; that nothing is too hard for God.)

Say: **Isn't it great to know that God can do anything? And because he can do anything, ★ sometimes God surprises us! When we're in a tough situation, we may not be able to think of a way out—but God can! Sarah couldn't think of a way she could have a baby when she was so old, but God did it! The missionaries at Kijabe couldn't think how one policeman and a barbed wire fence could protect them from attacking Mau Maus, but God knew what to do.**

We always need to remember that God is bigger, wiser, and more powerful than we are, so God can surprise us. Let's see if we can think of ways God might surprise kids today.

Form three groups and give each group one of the situation cards from the "God's Good Surprises" handout. Make sure you have a good balance of readers and nonreaders in each group.

Say: **Each group needs a reader who will read your situation aloud, an encourager who will encourage everyone to share ideas, and a reporter who will tell the whole class about your ideas. Brainstorm at least three ways God might surprise the people in your situation. You've got three minutes. Go!**

Circulate among groups as they work, encouraging discussion and offering ideas. Here are some possible outcomes for each situation.

Situation One: Alyssa might find a really great friend who lives on the same street her grandma does. If the grandma lives on a farm, Alyssa might be able to have the horse she's

Teacher Tip

Choose a kid-friendly Bible such as Group's Hands-On Bible® for use with the lessons.

always dreamed of. Alyssa might find a club at her new church where she makes lots of new friends.

Situation Two: Matt might find out that two of the kids are really nice after all; they've just been following the lead of another boy. The assistant principal might realize that he's put Matt in a difficult situation and decide to move Matt right away. Matt might discover that the boys aren't mean after all, and they could end up being friends.

Situation Three: A truck driver might stop and help the dad fix the car right on the spot. A policeman might radio for a tow truck so the car could get fixed quickly and the family could be on their way. The car might have broken down right in front of a farmhouse owned by people who are friendly and helpful.

After two minutes, clap your hands and announce that kids have one more minute for discussion. After one more minute, clap your hands and bring everyone together. Ask the reader from the first group to read that group's situation, and have the reporter tell the group's ideas of how God might surprise the person in that situation. Invite the rest of the class to add their ideas. Repeat this process for the second and third groups.

Say: **Congratulations! Those are great ideas. You're really catching on to the fact that even when things seem impossible, ★ sometimes God surprises us.**

COMMITMENT

Surprise Pop-Up

Say: **Let's make reminders to help us be on the lookout for God's surprises every day.**

Distribute photocopies of the "Surprise Pop-Up" handout. Be sure you've made a sample pop-up card before class so kids can see how the three-dimensional card works.

Set out markers, glitter glue, scissors, and tape. Encourage kids to decorate the handout creatively and then cut the paper in half horizontally on the solid line. The top half of the handout becomes the card base; have kids set it aside for a moment.

Have kids fold the bottom of the handout in half and then cut from point A to point B and unfold the present. Have them cut a slit on the solid line from the bottom of the page to the dotted line and fold forward on the dotted line. Show kids how to tape the bottom sections that are folded forward to the shaded area of the card base. When the card base is folded, the present disappears. When the card base is opened, the present pops up. As kids are working on their pop-up cards, encourage them to tell about times God has surprised them. Have kids who finish early help clean up the paper scraps and put the art supplies away.

When everyone is finished, have kids form pairs.

Say: **Tell your partner where you'll put this pop-up card so it can remind you to watch for God's good surprises.**

Give kids a moment to share. Then ask:

♦ **Why does God surprise us?** (Because God loves us; because God knows so much more than we do.)

♦ **Does God always make difficult situations turn out the way we want them to? Explain.** (No, because God is wiser than we are; no, not for me.)

Say: **God isn't like a genie or a fairy godmother, so God doesn't always make things turn out the way we wish they would. Then again, sometimes God makes things turn out better than we ever thought they could. The important thing to remember is that God is all-powerful—he can do anything. And God is all-wise—he knows what's best for us. And God's love for us is bigger than the universe, so we can always trust him to make things turn out for the best.**

CLOSING

God's Surprises

Ask:

♦ **What was the impossible problem Sarah faced in our Bible story today?** (She couldn't have a baby.)

Say: **We also talked about some big problems kids today might face, such as a parent losing a job, moving away from friends, scary things at school, and having a car break down. I wonder if anyone here today is facing a problem that seems impossible that you'd like to have us pray about.**

If your kids are open and comfortable with each other, invite them to share their concerns with the class. If kids aren't used to being together, they may prefer to talk to you individually after class.

Say: **It's great to know that we don't have to come up with solutions to problems that seem impossible. Our God is great and powerful and loving, and ★ sometimes God surprises us. Let's thank God for that right now.**

Pray: **Lord, thank you for the great God you are. Thank you for being wise and powerful and for loving us. Help us to look to you and trust you to surprise us. In Jesus' name, amen.**

Remind children to take their potatoes, straws, prizes, and pop-up surprise cards home. Encourage them to use these items to tell their families about today's lesson.

Teacher Tip

If you sense that a child is troubled about a problem, you can approach the child in a nonthreatening manner after class. Gently ask, "Is there anything you'd like to talk with me about?" Respect the child's right to refuse. Just by asking, you've shown that you're concerned, and you've laid the groundwork for the child to approach you in the future.

SARAH'S SURPRISE

(based on Genesis 18:1-15; 21:1-3)

I was sitting inside my tent one day
When three strangers passed our way.
(Walk three fingers across palm.)

My husband, Abraham, bowed low,
For these were important men, you know.
(Bow.)

He said, "Please rest and wash your feet
While my wife and I fix something to eat."

So they sat down beneath a tree,
And Abraham came to talk to me.

(Cup hands around mouth and whisper loudly.)
"Please make some bread. Be quick! Let's hurry!"
So I jumped up and worked in a flurry.

"Flour, salt, and a little yeast,
Now help me stir—we'll make a feast."
(Pretend to stir.)

Abraham cooked a tender roast.
Don't you think he's quite a fine host?
(Put hands on hips and nod proudly.)

The guests enjoyed the food we made
While Abraham stood close by in the shade.

"Where's your wife, Sarah?" one man asked.
When I heard my name, I stopped and gasped.
(Gasp.)

Abraham answered, "In the tent over there."
Then I began to listen with care.
(Cup hand to ear.)

"I'll come back next year," said guest number one.
"And when I come back, she'll have a son."
(Fold arms and nod.)

"A son?" I thought. "But I'm too old!
I'll never have a baby to hold."
(Shake head.)

"My husband and I are wrinkled and gray.
No child for us! No baby! No way!"

"A son? Oh, no! Ha-ha! Hee-hee!"
I felt the laughter rising in me.
(Hold stomach and laugh.)

"A son? At my age? It must be a joke!"
I laughed so hard I started to choke.

Laughter made tears roll down my cheek
(run finger down cheek),
But then our guest began to speak.

"Why does she laugh about having a son?
By this time next year, it will be done!"
(Shake finger.)

"I didn't laugh, sir." I was scared, so I lied.
"Oh yes, you did," our guest replied.
(Nod head.)

Finally our guests went on their way,
But I tell you, I'll never forget that day.
(Shake head.)

Can you tell what happened? I'll give you a clue.
What our visitor said really came true!

Before the year was past and done,
I gave birth to a beautiful son!
(Pretend to hold baby.)

You've never seen such a fine little boy.
He was Abraham's pride and joy.
(Fold arms and nod.)

We named him Isaac—that means "laughter."
Because we lived happily ever after.
(Cross hands over heart.)

Now listen to me because I am wise.
You've learned how God gave me a huge surprise.

And someday God may surprise you, too
(point at a child),
For there isn't anything God can't do.

GOD'S GOOD SURPRISES

Photocopy and cut apart the situations.

Alyssa was sure this was the worst day of her life. Her dad had lost his job a year ago. He'd found some temporary work, but it didn't pay very well. Finally Alyssa's parents decided to sell their house and move 300 miles away to live with Alyssa's grandma. Alyssa would have to go to a new school where she didn't know anyone.

How might God surprise Alyssa?

There had been a lot of trouble in the lunchroom at school lately, so the assistant principal decided to assign seats. "The seat you get today is where you'll stay for the rest of the year," he announced. Matt couldn't believe it when he was assigned to a table with some of the meanest kids in the whole school. "This is horrible," Matt thought. "I have to sit with these guys for the rest of the year!"

How might God surprise Matt?

Alex and Stephanie's parents had been promising all summer that the family would go on a canoe trip. Now they were finally on their way. But just an hour from home, their car broke down. "We'll never get our canoe trip," Alex moaned. "Why did this have to happen now?"

How might God surprise Alex and his family?

Published in *All-in-One Sunday School Volume 1* by Group Publishing, Inc., 1515 Cascade Ave., Loveland, CO 80538.

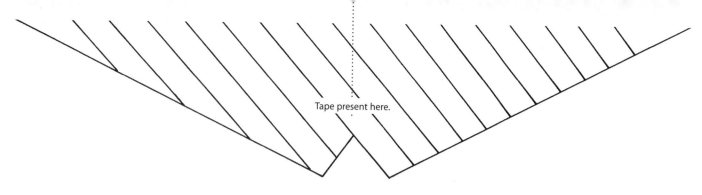

What is impossible with men is

POSSIBLE

with God
(from Luke 18:27).

B

SURPRISE!

A

LESSON

7

LESSON AIM

To help kids understand that ★ God wants us to be encouragers.

OBJECTIVES

Kids will

✓ observe how putdowns deflate a "balloon person,"
✓ listen to how putdowns harmed Abraham's his family,
✓ practice making encouraging comments, and
✓ prepare messages of encouragement for others.

YOU'LL NEED

❏ round balloons
❏ long balloons
❏ masking tape
❏ string
❏ markers
❏ straight pins
❏ an adult to play the role of Abraham (optional)
❏ bathrobe for Abraham's costume
❏ Bible
❏ overalls and shirt on a hanger
❏ newspapers
❏ photocopies of the "Talking Card" handout (p. 72)
❏ scissors
❏ pencils

BIBLE BASIS

Genesis 21:1-14

God shows us in this very early story of a family's struggle and eventual breakdown how damaging mockery and putdowns can be. God had promised to make Abraham the father of many nations. But for scores of years Abraham wasn't

able to become the father of even one child. Finally Sarah, Abraham's wife, urged Abraham to have a child with her servant Hagar. When Hagar became pregnant, she mocked Sarah, causing terrible heartache and discord in the household. Hagar eventually gave birth to Ishmael. But God told Abraham that Ishmael was not the son he had promised—Sarah would conceive in her old age and bear him a son.

When Sarah gave birth to Isaac, Ishmael must have felt cast off and displaced, even though Scripture says Abraham loved him. Ishmael's mockery of Isaac at a party given in Isaac's honor was the proverbial last straw. Sarah demanded—and got—immediate dismissal of Hagar and Ishmael from the family.

Ephesians 4:29

In this passage, Paul warns Christians against evil speaking, but then he goes on to state the same principle in a positive way: Say what encourages people and builds them up.

UNDERSTANDING YOUR KIDS

"Where did you come up with that outfit?" That comment has stuck with me since sixth grade. I can remember exactly what I was wearing, who said it, who witnessed it, where we were standing in the school, and what the weather was like!

To paraphrase a childish expression: Sticks and stones may break my bones, but bones heal in a few weeks. Putdowns will almost always hurt me and probably stick with me for years to come.

Putdowns are easy to understand. If my words cut someone down, then I'm suddenly bigger in comparison. Unfortunately, putdowns know no age limit. For kids at the lower end of your age-group a putdown may be something like, "Can't you even tie your shoes yet?" Older kids may come out with charming phrases like, "Don't be such a sleaze-ball."

The good news is putdowns and negative speech are habits—and habits can be changed. A positive spirit is as contagious as a negative one. This lesson gives you a chance to show kids it feels good to make others feel good—and it pleases God, as well.

The Lesson 😊

ATTENTION GRABBER

Hey, Mr. Balloon Man!

As kids arrive have them form groups of about five. Give each group one round balloon, four long balloons, tape, string and a marker. Explain that each group is to build a balloon person by blowing up the balloons and taping or tying them together. Groups can use the round balloon as the head and the four long balloons as arms and legs. Have kids use markers to give their balloon people faces.

Have groups bring their finished balloon people to the front. Say to one of the balloon people: **I think you're full of hot air.**

Follow the putdown with sticking a straight pin into one of the balloons. Give kids each a straight pin and invite kids to insult other groups' balloon people and to pop one balloon after each putdown.

After all the balloon people have been destroyed, ask:

♦ **What was this experience like for you?** (It felt terrible; it was fun at first, but when I saw my balloon person getting hurt I wanted to stop.)

♦ **How is this like what happens when people put others down?** (It feels like they stuck me with a pin; it feels like I shrink and become an ugly little blob.)

Say: **We know putdowns cause hurt and angry feelings. ★ God wants us to be encouragers. Today we're going to see how putdowns tore apart a Bible-times family. As a matter of fact, the father of that family is going to pay us a visit and tell us the sad story—right now!**

BIBLE STUDY

A Sad Day (Genesis 21:1-14)

Tell kids a very famous person from the Old Testament is going to visit your class. If you recruited an adult to play the part of Abraham, cue him to enter now.

Or you may choose to have one of your older boys play Abraham. Make sure you choose a good reader. Let the other kids use the bathrobe to dress him as a Bible-times character, and then welcome him to class with a round of applause. Have him read or recite the story "A Visit From Abraham" on page 70.

After Abraham makes his exit, ask:

♦ **Why do you think Ishmael acted that way?** (He was jealous of all the attention Isaac was getting.)

♦ **When have you felt jealous like Ishmael did?** Allow kids to respond.

♦ **What happens when we make fun of others?** (Their feelings get hurt; we get in trouble; they may try to get back at us by putting us down.)

Say: **Sometimes it feels good just for a minute when we put someone down. But the good feeling never lasts. And we usually end up paying for it in the end, just as Ishmael did. Let's see what the Bible has to say about putdowns. ★God wants us to be encouragers.**

Fold in half lengthwise and cut horizontal slit in the mouth.

LIFE APPLICATION

Stuffed With Affirmations

Have a volunteer read Ephesians 4:29 aloud. Bring out your overalls and shirt and a stack of newspapers. Hang the hanger with the clothes on a nail or over a door.

Say: **We saw how putdowns destroyed our balloon people. Now we're going to do just the opposite. We're going to build this person up by giving encouragement and saying things that make a person feel good.**

Wad up a piece of newspaper, stuff it into the shirt and say: **I'm glad you came to class today.**

Let kids take turns stuffing the figure with newspapers and saying one encouraging comment with each newspaper wad they stuff. Guide the process so the arms, legs and body each get some stuffing.

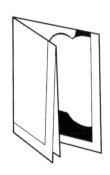

Open and fold in quarters with mouth on inside.

When the figure is well-stuffed, say: **Look at how the encouraging things we said have built up this person. Let's see if this works in real life.**

Have kids take turns standing in front of the class. Give the rest of the children 20 seconds to make positive comments about the person who's standing. After everyone—including you!—has received encouragement and affirmation, ask:

♦ **How did it feel to hear everyone's encouraging comments?** Allow kids to share their feelings.

Push lips out from center fold.

COMMITMENT

Encouraging Words

Say: **We don't want all these encouraging words to stay here in our class. We want to encourage each other after class and during the week, too. ★ God wants us to be encouragers. We're going to make cards to give to people this week.**

Give kids each a photocopy of the "Talking Card" handout, a

A VISIT FROM ABRAHAM

Hello, children. It's nice to see all of you here today. I've always loved children. But for a long time I didn't think I'd have any of my own. You see, I was even older than your grandparents when my first son was born. Since my wife Sarah had been unable to have children, I had a son with my wife's servant Hagar. That was a common practice back in our day.

I was so proud of young Ishmael. He was a fine lad. But poor Sarah, my wife, longed for a son of her own. We prayed for years that God would send us a son. And it finally happened when Sarah was over 90 years old! We were so happy when our son was born we named him Isaac, which means laughter.

But things didn't stay happy around our house for too long. Ishmael was used to being the only son, and he was jealous of Isaac. He teased Isaac and mocked him all the time. And every time it happened, Isaac would run to his mother and complain. Then Sarah would come to me and say: "I've had it with Ishmael. He's always putting Isaac down. One day he'll go too far."

And that's exactly what happened. One day we were having a big birthday party for Isaac. Ishmael hung around the tent, picking at Isaac and making fun of him all day. Finally Sarah blew up.

"That's it!" she shouted. "I want Hagar and her son out of here today. Ishmael has made fun of Isaac for the last time. I want them out of here now!"

It was awful. I loved both my sons. But I could see Sarah was right. Ishmael would just keep making trouble as long as he was around. So early the next morning I packed up some food and water and sent Hagar and Ishmael away.

I cried as I watched them go, but I knew God would take care of them. If only Ishmael could have learned to treat Isaac nicer, this could have been different...

(Abraham wanders away sadly shaking his head.)

pair of scissors, and a pencil. Demonstrate how to fold and cut the card so the lips move.

Have kids form pairs, younger kids with older kids, to work on their cards. Have partners discuss who to send the card to and what message of encouragement to write in the speech balloon. Let older kids do the writing for younger ones whose writing skills aren't yet developed.

CLOSING

Boisterous Buildups

Have kids stand in a circle holding their completed cards. Explain that on the count of three, kids will make their cards talk all at once, saying the encouraging message that's written on them.

Say: **That sounds terrific. Let's remember to use words that build people up, not put them down.**

Bring the stuffed-overall person into the center of the circle. Close with a prayer similar to this one: **Dear Lord, thank you for the encouraging words we've all heard from each other today. Help us to keep building each other up. In Jesus' name, amen.**

Remind kids to show their talking cards to their parents and then to send the cards to the people they thought of when they wrote their encouraging messages.

"When you talk, do not say harmful things,
but say what people need—words that will
help others become stronger. Then what you
say will do good to those who listen to you"
(Ephesians 4:29, NIV).

I just had to tell you …

LESSON AIM

To help kids understand that ★ God wants us to be helpful and kind even when no one else is watching.

OBJECTIVES

Kids will

✓ play a game and guess who's being affirmed,
✓ hear how a young woman's act of kindness caused Abraham's servant to choose her for Isaac's bride,
✓ create treats to share, and
✓ plan ways to be helpful and kind to people they don't usually notice.

YOU'LL NEED

❏ slips of paper
❏ pencils
❏ a basket
❏ a bottle of bubbles
❏ a photocopy of the "Eliezer's Journey" script (p. 80)
❏ an adult male volunteer to play the role of Eliezer (optional)
❏ a costume for Eliezer—a robe, sandals, towels, neckties
❏ quilt batting for a beard, double-sided tape (optional)
❏ Bible
❏ plain sugar cookies (homemade or from the store)
❏ canned frosting
❏ paper plates
❏ cookie decorations such as cinnamon hearts, small gumdrops, skinny licorice whips, and colorful sprinkles
❏ plastic knives
❏ sandwich bags
❏ photocopy of the "Sneaky Treat Tags' handout (p.82)
❏ scissors   ❏ stapler   ❏ ribbon
*Always check for allergies before serving snacks.

Teacher Tip

This lesson works well with an intergenerational class. You may wish to invite families to join you for this session.

all-in-one
SUNDAY
SCHOOL

BIBLE BASIS

Genesis 24:1-67

When Abraham grew old, he began to be concerned about finding the right wife for his son, Isaac. Determined not to have Isaac marry a local Canaanite woman who would have come from a background of idol worship, Abraham sent a trusted servant back to Haran to find a woman from his own family. (This servant may have been Eliezer, who is mentioned in Genesis 15:2 as the probable recipient of Abraham's wealth if he were to die without a child of his own.)

The servant loaded 10 camels with supplies and gifts and took off on the long trip. As the servant neared the town where Abraham's relatives lived, he paused and prayed for God's help and blessing in identifying the young woman who would marry Isaac. Before he even finished praying, Rebekah came to the well! When the servant asked her for a drink, she gave it, then graciously offered to draw water for his camels as well. Her act of kindness was exactly the sign the servant had prayed for!

Rebekah readily agreed to travel back to Canaan and marry her unknown cousin. And so she came to take her place in history as an ancestress of Christ. It was Rebekah's helpfulness to a stranger that helped identify her as God's choice to become Isaac's wife. Though it was common courtesy to offer a drink to a thirsty traveler, Rebekah went beyond the expected when she offered to provide as much water as the camels would drink. And she did it with no expectation of reward—she was completely unaware of the servant's identity and the rich gifts he was about to offer.

Matthew 25:34-40

Expectations for giving and receiving hospitality in Bible times were higher than most of us today would enjoy dealing with. Sharing the resources of the home was a binding obligation. But Jesus gave new meaning to offering the basic necessities of food, drink, and clothing when he said, "When you did it to one of the least of these my brothers and sisters, you were doing it to me" (Matthew 25:40). We Christians today would do well to go out of our way to offer help and kindness to those who usually escape our notice.

When it comes to being helpful and kind, kids can be motivated more by self-interest than intrinsic goodness. If someone they want to impress is watching, they'll bend over backward to help. What greater honor can there be than to do an errand for the teacher? But when children have an opportunity to be helpful to someone who's not important to them, when no one's watching, it may be more difficult to find the motivation to act.

Use this lesson to teach kids that their small acts of helpfulness and caring are important to God.

The Lesson 😊

ATTENTION GRABBER

Bubbles of Kindness

As kids arrive, have them write their names on slips of paper and drop them into a basket. Then form pairs, matching younger children with older ones. New children to the class should be placed with partners who know everyone else.

Have partners sit facing each other, next to other pairs, forming a double circle. Pass the basket, and have everyone draw a name. If kids draw their own names or their partners' names, have them put the slips back and draw again. When everyone has drawn a name, say: **Please keep the names you have a secret until I tell you how and when to reveal them. You're going to say something kind about the person whose name you're holding—but you're not going to say who it is. You and your partner can work together to finish this sentence: "The thing I really like about this person is..." And you need to say something more than "He's nice" or "She's sweet." You might say, "The thing I really like about this person is that this person is always friendly and helpful," or "that this person always says something funny and cheers everyone up."**

Hold up a bottle of bubbles. **When I call on you to tell about the person whose name you've drawn, I'll hand you this bottle of bubbles. You'll tell about the person; then the rest of us will try to guess who you were talking about. When we guess the right person, you'll go to that person and blow bubbles over his or her head. Then you'll hand that person the bottle of bubbles, and he or she will be the next to talk.**

Here's an important rule: In this game we'll say only good things about people—things that will make us all feel good. Okay—go to a quiet spot with your partner. I'll give you two minutes to plan what you're going to say.

Let partners scatter around the room to plan their affirmations. Circulate among partners to make sure everyone comes up with something positive and complimentary. After two minutes, call time and have everyone sit in a circle. Give the bottle of bubbles to an outgoing child to begin. When the group guesses the identity of the affirmed person, have the first child blow bubbles over his or her head and then pass the bubbles on. Continue until everyone has shared an affirmation. Then take the bottle of bubbles, and ask:

♦ **What was it like to hear nice things without knowing who they were about?** (Cool—I kept wondering if it was about me; it was fun to guess the person.)

♦ **How often do you go out of your way to say nice things to people?** (Not very often; I usually try to say nice things to my friends.)

Say: **It's easy to be kind and caring to people we know and like in a situation like this one where everyone is watching. And we sometimes go out of our way to be helpful to teachers or other leaders. But the Bible teaches us that it's important to be kind to people who don't seem to be especially important—people we may not even know. ★ God wants us to be helpful and kind even when no one else is watching. Today's Bible story is about a young woman who did just that, and she became part of one of the greatest and most famous families of all time.**

BIBLE STUDY

Eliezer's Journey

Before class, arrange for an older man to visit your class in the role of Eliezer. Give him a photocopy of the script, "Eliezer's Journey." Have him create a Bible-times costume from a bathrobe and sandals. Suggest a towel for a headpiece and strips of fabric or old neckties for a belt and a headband.

If you're planning an intergenerational class, choose one of the men who's present to play Eliezer. Make sure you choose someone who's comfortable reading a script in front of a group. Give him the script at the start of class so he can quickly read over it. When it's time for the story, kids will love helping to dress him in an improvised costume. If he's beardless, let kids use some quilt batting or fiberfill and double-sided tape to help him grow a beard right on the spot!

Tell your helper whether you'll sing "Father Abraham" as part of the story—it's mentioned in an optional section of the script.

Introduce him by saying: **I'm glad to tell you that we have a fascinating guest speaker today. He'll be telling you the Bible story. His name is Eliezer** (el-ih-EE-zur), **and he is the most trusted servant of Abraham. Eliezer was almost like a son to Abraham—but I'll let him tell the story. So let's give a hearty welcome to Eliezer!**

Lead kids in clapping and cheering; then encourage them to be attentive listeners.

After Eliezer finishes his story, have everyone give your helper a big round of applause. Then ask:

♦ **How would you like to have your mom or dad or uncle pick out a husband or wife for you?** (Yuck!; no way; I'm never getting married.)

♦ **What qualities was Eliezer hoping to find in a wife for Isaac?** (Someone who was kind and helpful; someone nice.)

♦ **How did Eliezer know for sure that Rebekah was the**

one God had chosen for Isaac? (Because he prayed; because she gave him a drink and gave water for all of his camels, too.)

Say: ★ **God wants us to be helpful and kind even when no one else is watching. Rebekah was helpful to Abraham's servant and was chosen to be one of the most famous brides in the Bible. But her actions showed that she would have been helpful and kind even if there had been no reward at all. Because she married into Abraham's family, she became Jesus' great-great-great-great—well, I don't know exactly how many "greats" there are—grandmother.**

Jesus was born about 2,000 years after Abraham and Isaac. And he taught how important it is to show kindness to all people. Let's read Jesus' words in Matthew 25:34-40. Have a volunteer look up and read those verses aloud. Then ask:

♦ **What did Jesus mean by "the least of my brothers and sisters"?** (People who no one really knows; poor people.)

♦ **Who are the "least of these" in our world today?** (People in poor countries; people who live on the street; people who are unpopular.)

LIFE APPLICATION

Sneaky Treats

Say: **One fun way to show kindness when no one is looking is to slip someone a fabulous treat, then sneak away.**

♦ **What would you do if you found a treat with your name on it, but you didn't know who gave you the treat?** (I'd look around to see if I could catch the person who left it; I'd wonder about who left it; I'd have a good feeling because someone cared for me.)

Say: **Let's get started making our Sneaky Treats. Since these treats look so amazingly wonderful, you'll be making one to eat yourselves and one to give away.**

Set out plain sugar cookies, plastic knives, paper plates, canned frosting, sandwich bags, and your choice of decorations such as cinnamon hearts, small gumdrops, skinny licorice whips, and colorful sprinkles. Have kids make a practice cookie—the one they'll eat—and then a masterpiece cookie—the one they'll give away.

As kids work, circulate among them asking about who will receive their sneaky treat, why they chose that person, and when and how they will make their sneaky delivery.

When the masterpiece cookies are finished, have kids put their cookies in a sandwich bag, add the name of the recipient to a Sneaky Treat Tag, and staple the tag and a ribbon to the sandwich bag.

♦ **Why we are giving away these Sneaky Treats?** (Because God wants us to be helpful and kind even when no one is watching.)

Say: **Good luck on your Sneaky Treat mission!**

COMMITMENT

The Least of These

Have kids form trios for the following discussion questions. (It's fine to have one or two groups of four if that's the way your numbers work out.) Pause after each question to allow for discussion time.

♦ **Tell about someone you didn't know who did something helpful and kind for you.** (A man stopped to help us change a flat tire; a neighbor helped me when I fell off my bike.)

♦ **Why does God want us to be helpful and kind, even when no one else is watching?** (Because God sees us even if no one else does; because that's how we show God's love.)

♦ **Who is someone you see from time to time who is like the "least of these" Jesus talks about in Matthew 25?** (A kid at school who doesn't have any friends; an older man who comes to our church.)

♦ **How could you use something you made or learned today to be helpful and kind to that person?** (I could share a cookie with him; I could give her a note saying I'd like to be friends.)

After trios have discussed the last question, call everyone together and say: **I'd like to hear about some of the interesting answers you came up with in your trios.**

Allow several participants to share.

CLOSING

Kindly Pop My Bubble

Say: ★ **God wants us to be helpful and kind, even when no one else is watching. Remember, even if no one else is watching, Jesus is. Jesus told us that when we do something kind for even the most unimportant person, it's like doing it for him. I hope you'll think about that this week when you see an older person who's having a difficult time getting around, when you see a child who's frightened or confused, or when an unpopular person at school is sitting all alone in the lunchroom.**

I'm going to blow some bubbles in the air. I'd like you to try to pop them all before they hit the ground. Each time you

ELIEZER'S JOURNEY

A wife! I had to find a wife! Not for me, mind you, but for my master's son, Isaac. I'm sure you've heard of my master. He's one of the most famous people in the Bible. His name is Abraham.

[Optional: You know that song about Father Abraham? Would you like to sing it right now? Let's do! I think this nice person right here will help lead it.]

Abraham waited years and years and years for the son God had promised. In fact, he was 100 years old when Isaac was born, and Sarah, his wife, was over 90! When the time finally came to choose a wife for Isaac, Abraham needed my help. In my day, young men and women didn't go on dates or send Valentines or anything like that. Their parents decided who they would marry. I think that's a good idea, don't you?

So one day Abraham called me in and said, "Eliezer, I want you to make me a promise. It's time to choose a wife for Isaac, but I don't want a Canaanite woman from around here. I want you to go back to my home country of Haran, far to the north, and choose a wife for Isaac from my own people." You see, the Canaanites who lived around us were idol worshippers. Abraham wanted Isaac's wife to be someone who would love God. Abraham also wanted me to promise not to take Isaac back to the old country. He knew that God had promised to make a new nation right here in Canaan.

Let me tell you, that was a lot to promise! But Abraham assured me that an angel would go before me and help me choose a wife for Isaac. So I agreed. I loaded up 10 camels with supplies and all kinds of wonderful gifts for the bride-to-be. And I took off on a month-long journey of more than 600 miles back to Haran, the land we had left so long ago.

When I got there, I prayed like crazy that God would let me know which was the right young woman. As I came to the town where Abraham's family lived, it was near sunset, and the young women were coming out to the well to draw water during the cool of the day. I prayed, "God, I'm standing here by this spring, and all the young women of the town are coming. When I ask a girl for a drink from her water jar, please let her say, 'Drink, and I'll draw water for your camels, too.' Then I'll know that she's the one for Isaac."

Just then a very lovely young lady came to the well. I rushed to catch up with her.

"Please give me a little water from your jar," I said.

"Please help yourself," she answered, "and I'll draw water for your camels, too, until they've all had enough to drink."

The Lord be praised! She answered just as I had prayed. She was so very kind to offer to draw so much water for a stranger like me, for her water jar was heavy, and my camels were thirsty. This was just the kind of young woman who would make a wonderful wife for Isaac!

Her name was Rebekah. I asked about her family and discovered that she was related to Abraham. Her family invited me to have dinner and spend the night with them. I gave Rebekah beautiful gold jewelry and gifts from my master. Then she agreed to go back to Canaan with me and marry Isaac. God be praised!

We made the long journey back to Canaan, and Isaac came out to meet us. It was love at first sight! My master, Abraham, was so pleased to hear how God had helped me find Rebekah because of her act of kindness.

pop a bubble, shout out one kind, helpful thing you'll do this week. Ready? Here we go!

Blow several strong puffs of bubbles in different directions. If you have adults in your class, make sure you aim some of the bubbles toward them! Then gather everyone for prayer.

Pray: **Dear Lord, please help us scatter acts of kindness all around us this week. Help us to remember that you want us to be helpful and kind even when no one else is watching,** because you're always watching. Help us show friendship in your name to people we usually don't even notice. In Jesus' name, amen.

SNEAKY TREAT BAG

Cut out each tag around the solid line.

LESSON AIM

To help kids understand that ★ God forgives us as we forgive others.

OBJECTIVES

Kids will

✓ experience frustration setting up dominoes,
✓ learn how Jacob and Esau forgave each other,
✓ understand that God wants them to accept his forgiveness and pass it on to others, and
✓ ask God's help in forgiving others.

YOU'LL NEED

❏ 2 to 4 sets of dominoes
❏ 2 adults to play the roles of Jacob and Esau (optional)
❏ bathrobes, sandals, and towels for costumes
❏ photocopies of the "Twin Troubles" script (p. 86)
❏ Bibles
❏ pencil
❏ photocopies of the "Cup of Forgiveness" handout (p. 91)
❏ 8-inch squares of paper
❏ a pitcher of water

BIBLE BASIS

Genesis 25–33

The story of Jacob and Esau is a story of grace. Sibling rivalry and parental favoritism created an ugly environment of trickery and hatred between the twin sons of Isaac. But God intervened and used these less-than-perfect heroes to perpetuate the Messianic line begun by Abraham.

After years of hatred and estrangement, the reunion of Jacob and Esau is nothing less than miraculous. Jacob had

all-in-one
SUNDAY
SCHOOL

stolen Esau's two most precious possessions: the birthright and blessing of the firstborn. During their years of living apart, Esau had plenty of time to nurse his grief and hatred.

But no blood was shed, no hard words spoken. "Esau ran to meet him and embrace him, threw his arms around his neck, and kissed him. And they both wept" (Genesis 33:4). What a beautiful, touching scene!

Our God is a God of grace and mercy. The mercy God shows us, he also requires of us.

1 Peter 4:8

When people intentionally hurt us, our first human reaction may be to defend ourselves. Our second reaction is almost always to think of ways to strike back.

People who know God know that the healing of a broken relationship is far more powerful and gratifying than revenge. Love is stronger than hate, and in the lives of God's people, love must always prevail.

UNDERSTANDING YOUR KIDS

"No fair!" How many times have you heard that from your students? Kids have a strong sense of justice, especially when they're the victims! And when they don't think justice is being served, their objections will come through loud and clear.

For younger children, forgiveness can be a confusing issue. When they're wronged, they want justice and they want it now. When a parent or teacher fails to exact a satisfactory punishment, they're upset. A young child often learns the best lessons about mercy and forgiveness when he or she is the wrongdoer—the one who broke the plate, hit a friend, or made the baby cry with an unkind word or action.

Older children may have entered the "grudge zone" where it's cool to run in cliques and put down their enemies. Kids in the middle grades need to be challenged to put themselves in other people's shoes and to respond in love.

That's a big order—one that many adults find difficult. But it's what God requires of us, and, in his grace, empowers us to do.

The Lesson 😊

ATTENTION GRABBER

Knock Me Down

As kids arrive, assign them to one of two groups. Keep the balance of younger and older students the same in each group. Give both groups a set or two of dominoes and challenge them to make a design with the dominoes that will fall over when one of the dominoes is pushed.

Visit the groups as work progresses. When a group is nearly done, pretend to adjust one of the dominoes and "accidentally" knock over the entire arrangement. Apologize; then back away from the scene of the accident straight into the other group's dominoes. Apologize again; then call a halt to the work and ask:

♦ **What did you think when I knocked over your dominoes and ruined your hard work?** (I couldn't believe you did that; it was frustrating.)

♦ **What would you think about me if I knocked over the dominoes by accident—just because I was clumsy?** (I wouldn't feel so bad; I wouldn't be mad at you.)

♦ **What would you think if you knew I knocked over the dominoes on purpose and that I'd keep knocking them over again and again?** (I might cry; I'd probably get mad at you; I'd quit trying to set them up.)

♦ **If I said I was sorry would you still be mad at me?** (Maybe; I'm not sure; not if you never did it again.)

Say: **It can be hard to forgive people, especially if they do hurtful things on purpose, and most especially if they do them again and again. Today we're going to learn that ★ God forgives us as we forgive others. Later in our class we'll work with the dominoes again—and this time I promise not to knock them over! Now let's listen to a story of two brothers who had a lot to forgive.**

BIBLE STUDY

Twin Troubles (Genesis 25:27-34; 27:1-45; 32:9-21; 33:1-4)

You may want to invite two adults from your congregation to read the roles of Jacob and Esau. Simple costumes such as bathrobes, sandals, and towels wrapped with fabric strips for headgear will add to the effect when two Bible characters suddenly appear in your class to tell the Bible story.

TWIN TROUBLES

Esau: I'm Esau. My brother Jacob and I are twins, but I was the first to be born. That gave me the right to get almost all my father's money and land. My father is really proud of me because I'm a great hunter.

Jacob: I'm Jacob. One thing I can tell you about my twin brother Esau is that he's not too smart. One day he was out hunting and came back really hungry. I had just finished fixing a pot of soup. It smelled good, and Esau wanted some right away. So I said, "Sure, you can have the soup if you'll give me your rights as the firstborn son." Esau agreed. I couldn't believe it. He traded away all his rights as firstborn son for a pot of soup!

Esau: One day when my father was very old, he called me in and asked me to go hunting and prepare him a meal of delicious meat. He told me that after he had eaten the meal I prepared, he would give me his blessing—the one thing Jacob hadn't taken from me.

Jacob: So while Esau went off to hunt, my mother prepared a meal of goat meat. My father couldn't see very well, so we thought we could trick him into giving me his blessing if I pretended to be Esau. It worked! My father gave me the blessing for the oldest son before Esau got back from his hunting trip.

Esau: I hurried back from my hunting trip and prepared a tasty meal for my father. Then I took it to him, only to discover that he had just given his blessing to my scheming brother, Jacob. What a dirty trick! I decided right then that I would kill Jacob.

Jacob: My mother heard about Esau's plans to kill me, so she sent me far away to my uncle's house. Saying goodbye to my parents was hard because I didn't know if I'd ever see them again. I lived many years at my uncle's house. I got married and had a big family. But I longed to return to my old home. Still...Esau had threatened to kill me. And who could blame him? I cheated him out of all of his rights as firstborn son.

Esau: Many years passed. One day I looked up and saw well-dressed servants coming toward me bringing flocks of goats, sheep, camels, cows, and donkeys. They said they were from my brother, Jacob. So Jacob was on his way home. I'd wondered for a long time if I'd ever see him again.

Or, you may choose two kids who are good readers to take the roles of Jacob and Esau.

In either case, assign half the children to belong to Jacob's group and the other half to belong to Esau's. Have the Jacob and Esau characters stand facing each other, with their groups behind them.

Say: **Our Bible story comes from the book of Genesis. It's about two brothers—twins—who didn't get along very well.**

As the characters read through the "Twin Troubles" script, encourage the kids in both groups to cheer for their characters.

At the end of the story, hand out Bibles and have everyone look up Genesis 33:4. Be sure to pair nonreaders with older kids who can find the verse and point out the words. Have a volunteer from each group read the verse aloud together with the other group's volunteer. Then have the Jacob and Esau characters shake hands or hug each other as the rest of the kids hug or shake hands with kids from the opposite group.

Ask:

♦ **How did the ending of this story surprise you?** (I expected them to fight; I've heard it before.)

♦ **What would you have done if you'd been in Esau's shoes?** (I'd have chased Jacob away; I'd have forgiven him if he'd asked me to; I'm not sure.)

♦ **Why didn't Esau try to kill Jacob?** (Because God helped him forgive Jacob; because a long time had passed, and Esau realized he still loved his brother.)

Say: **Sometimes it's hard to forgive people who do mean things to us. But the Bible tells us that ★ God forgives us as we forgive each other. Let's find out more about what that means.**

LIFE APPLICATION

No Tricks Allowed

Form three groups. Make sure you have an older boy or girl in each group.

Say: **You're going to help me make up a story. I'll take turns asking each group to give me a word for our story. When it's your group's turn, make a huddle and then call out the word you choose. I'll tell you exactly what kind of word I need. When we've filled in all the blanks, I'll read our story out loud.**

Jot down kids responses in the blanks of the "Championship Trick" story on the next page. Then read the story aloud, inserting the kids' words as you read.

Teacher Tip

Depending on the age of your kids, you may or may not experience "gender repulsion" in your group. Kids may be reluctant to touch or even work with those of the opposite sex. If this is the case with your group, stick to handshakes rather than hugs!

Teacher Tip

Encourage kids to use good judgment in choosing words that will make the story interesting, but nothing negative or in poor taste.

CHAMPIONSHIP TRICK

It was the bottom of the ninth. The _____ (town) Hornets and the _____ (another town) Stingers were in a fight for the _____ (name of animal) league championship. The game had been really _____ (adjective), and everyone was feeling _____ (adjective). _____ (boy's name) up to bat. The crowd grew even more _____ (adjective). The Hornets fans were yelling, "_____ (verb), Hornets, _____ (same verb)." The Stingers fans were yelling, "_____ (verb), Stingers, _____ (same verb)." _____ (same boy) _____ (past tense of verb) the bat and stared _____ (adverb) at the pitcher. Two men on, two outs. This was it—the championship.

The pitch _____ (past tense of verb) in. _____ (same boy) swung. The bat hit the ball with a loud _____ (sound). The ball _____ (past tense of verb) into center field—a base hit! _____ (same boy) _____ (past tense of verb) down the line toward first base. But suddenly he _____ (past tense of verb) to the ground with a thud. While _____ (same boy) was at bat, the catcher had untied both his shoelaces, causing him to trip. The _____ (adjective) center fielder threw the ball to the first baseman well before _____ (same boy) arrived. The game was over—ended on a _____ (adjective) trick.

Read the story aloud and enjoy a good laugh. Then say: **That's pretty funny, but when someone hurts you or plays a trick on you in real life, it's not funny at all. In fact, you may feel like doing something to get back at that person. But let's read about what God wants us to do.**

Have a volunteer read 1 Peter 4:8. Then have another volunteer summarize the verse in his or her own words.

Say: **In your groups, tell about a time you were able to forgive someone and how it felt to do that. Let's have two rules: Don't use people's real names and don't tell about anyone in this room.**

Travel from group to group as kids share. After two or three minutes, say: **Now let's do something fun that shows us how God's forgiveness works.**

COMMITMENT

Cup of Forgiveness

Distribute photocopies of the "Cup of Forgiveness" handout and 8-inch squares of paper. Have everyone watch as you demonstrate how to fold the cup. Then have kids work together in their groups as they each fold their own cups. Encourage kids who are quick with their paper folding to help others complete their cups.

Then form one large circle. Pour water from a pitcher into your cup as you say: **Forgiveness comes from God. ★ God forgives us as we forgive others.** As you say "others," pour the water from your cup into the cup of the person on your right. Have that person repeat the sentence "God forgives us as we forgive others," and pour the water into the next person's cup. Continue in that manner around the circle.

If someone spills the water, refill his or her cup from the pitcher and say: **God's forgiveness never runs dry.** Then continue until the water comes back to you.

Say: **God's forgiveness works just like our circle. We receive forgiveness from God, then we pass that forgiveness on to others. Our circle of forgiveness becomes a circle of love. Hold your cup in both hands and think of one person you need to forgive. Silently pray and ask God to help you love and forgive that person.**

After a few moments of silence, pray: **Thank you, Lord, for your gift of forgiveness. Help us pass that gift on to others. In Jesus' name, amen.**

CLOSING

Circle of Love

Say: **Remember my promise that we'd do something more with the dominoes? Now is the time! Let's make one big circle using all the dominoes and see if we can all get inside the circle without knocking them down.**

Have everyone step inside the completed circle. Ask:

♦ **What did we learn today?** (God forgives us as we forgive others).

Say: **Let's shout that aloud together, then** [name the youngest child] **can push the first domino in our circle of love.**

Encourage kids to keep their cups as reminders of God's forgiveness.

CUP OF FORGIVENESS

"Continue to show deep love for each other, for love covers a multitude of sins" (1 Peter 4:8).

1. Fold a square of paper in half, forming a triangle that points upard.

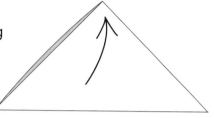

2. Fold the bottom right corner to the top left edge.

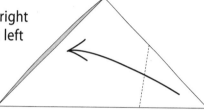

3. Turn the paper over. Fold the bottom right corner to the top left edge.

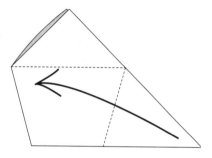

4. Fold the top front flap into the front pocket. Fold the back flap into the back pocket.

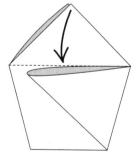

5. Here's your finished cup!

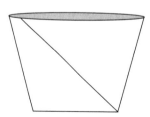

10

LESSON AIM

To help kids learn that ★ families are important to God.

OBJECTIVES

Kids or families will

✓ do family role-plays with their wrists tied together,
✓ learn what effect bragging and jealousy had on Joseph's family,
✓ explore biblical ways to solve family problems, and
✓ commit to showing God's love in their families.

YOU'LL NEED

❑ 12-inch lengths of string or ribbon
❑ markers
❑ large paper grocery bags
❑ T-shirts
❑ sweat pants or shorts
❑ Hershey's Kisses chocolates*
❑ towelettes or damp washcloths in sandwich bags
❑ scissors
❑ Bibles
❑ Bible costumes (optional)
❑ slips of paper
❑ a pencil
❑ photocopies of the "Funtastic Families" handout (p. 98)
❑ star stickers

*Always check for allergies before serving snacks.

Teacher Tip

This lesson works well with an intergenerational class. You may wish to invite whole families to join you for this session.

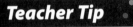
all-in-one
SUNDAY
SCHOOL

BIBLE BASIS

Genesis 37:1-36

There's no such thing as a perfect family. From the very beginning of Scripture, God points out human weaknesses that led to family feuds and the tragic consequences that followed. The stories of the patriarchs are filled with scheming, jealousy, and even murder.

When we look at the story of Joseph and his brothers, we probably get a little angry with Jacob for his obvious favoritism. But think back to Jacob's family of origin. Jacob was favored by his mother, Rebekah, while Isaac preferred Esau, Jacob's twin. Rebekah and Jacob schemed together to steal Esau's birthright. Pain and dysfunction went from generation to generation in ancient times, just as they do today.

God has a better plan—a plan of forgiveness and healing. This lesson will deal with Joseph's perseverance and reconciliation with his brothers.

Ephesians 4:29–5:1

Unfortunately, most of us have a perverse tendency to save our worst behavior for those we love the most. These verses encourage a thoughtful, loving, forgiving mind-set. Help kids understand that home is the best place to learn to practice Christlike behavior.

UNDERSTANDING YOUR KIDS

Families come in all sizes and shapes. You'll need to be careful to see that kids from every kind of family situation feel accepted and "normal" in your class.

You're probably aware that kids whose parents are divorced often feel responsible for the problems in their families. It will be especially important to tactfully protect these kids from feeling singled out in any way during this lesson.

Kids can't be responsible for what other people in their families do. But children can make a positive difference in their families by making a commitment to love, forgive, and interact positively with the people in their homes.

all-in-one
SUNDAY
SCHOOL

The Lesson 😊

ATTENTION GRABBER

Stuck Together

As people arrive, assign them to families. Make families as small as two or three, and as large as six or seven. If you've invited whole families to an intergenerational class, scramble them so no two members of a real family end up together.

Have the families you created sit together in a circle. Distribute 12-inch lengths of string or ribbon and have family members tie their wrists together with the people on their left and right.

When all the families are tied together in their own circles, give each family a marker and a large paper grocery bag containing a T-shirt, sweat pants or shorts, several Hershey's Kisses chocolates, and a towelette or damp washcloth in a sandwich bag.

Say: **Decide what you want your family's last name to be, and write it in big letters on your paper bag.**

Acknowledge each of the family names by saying, "Oh, here are the Joneses" or "I see we have the Oglethorpe family here today. Welcome!"

Then say: **We're about to embark on a family adventure. I'll tell you what to do. You'll find all the things you need in your handy-dandy family bag. But don't look in the bag until I tell you what you need.**

Give families this series of commands:

♦ **Choose one person to be the baby. Dress the baby. Take the T-shirt out of the bag and slip it over the baby's head. Then find the sweat pants or shorts and help the baby put them on.**

♦ **Eat breakfast. Take the chocolates out of the bag. Each person will unwrap one chocolate and feed it to the person on his or her left.**

♦ **Drive to work and school. Stand up together and walk clockwise around the room until you come back to your original spot.**

♦ **Drive home. Stand up together and walk counterclockwise around the room until you come back to your original spot.**

♦ **Eat dinner. Unwrap another chocolate and feed it to the person on your right.**

♦ **Clean up after dinner. Take the washcloth or towelette out of the sandwich bag and gently wipe the hands of the person on your left.**

After the families have completed all these activities, give an older child in each family a pair of scissors to cut the family members apart. Have families put their props back in their bags. Then gather everyone in a circle. Ask:

♦ **What was difficult about this activity?** (It was hard to do everything when we were all tied together.)

♦ **How were you able to accomplish everything I asked you to do?** (By working together; by cooperating.)

♦ **What happened if you couldn't agree on how to do something?** (It took us longer; we had to agree.)

♦ **How was this experience like what happens in your real families at home?** (We all have to work together; we have to help each other; we have to think about what other people need.)

Say: **As I watched you work in your family groups, it looked like you were having lots of fun. But sometimes you looked frustrated, and you had to work hard. It's the same with our families in real life. We have good times and hard times, and we all need to keep working together. Today we're going to learn some of what the Bible says about families because ★ families are important to God.**

BIBLE STUDY

The Case of the Missing Brother (Genesis 37)

Set up a readers theater by placing four chairs at the corners of a large square. Choose one person to be Joseph; one to be Joseph's father, Jacob; one person to be Reuben; and one to be Judah. Ask each character to be seated in one of the chairs. Have everyone else sit in the middle of the square and take the role of the other brothers.

Say: **Let's open our Bibles to Genesis 37 to find out what happened to a very important family in the Bible. I'll be the narrator. I'll nod to the people playing Joseph, Jacob, Reuben, and Judah when it's their turn to read. The rest of you will be Joseph's other brothers. Every time you hear me read the word "brothers," say, "Mumble, mumble, mumble," as if you're angry.**

Read all of Genesis 37, cuing characters to read their parts at the appropriate times. Encourage the characters to read dramatically and add action to their parts.

After the reading, call for a big round of applause. Then ask:

♦ **Who do you feel sorry for in this story?** (Joseph, because he was sold as a slave; Jacob, because he lost his favorite son; the brothers, because their father played favorites.)

♦ **Whose fault was it that Joseph was sold as a slave?** (Joseph's, because he bragged; the brothers', because they were jealous; Jacob's, because he didn't treat all his children the same.)

Teacher Tip

You may want to provide a special jacket for Joseph to wear and bathrobes as Bible-time scostumes for the other characters. If you have adults in your class, you might choose adults to take the parts of the narrator and Jacob. That would free you to sit with the kids and coach the other readers.

Say: **When there's trouble in a family, we usually try to pin the blame on someone else. But saying it's someone else's fault doesn't solve anything. Usually everyone plays some part in the problem, just like in Joseph's family.** Ask:

◆ **Those of you who read special parts, what could your character have done to prevent what happened to Joseph at the end of this story?** (Jacob could have shown all his sons that he loved them; Joseph could have kept from bragging and showing off his special coat; Judah could have talked with the brothers about settling the problem a better way.)

Say: **When there's a family problem, everyone can work together to solve it. And that pleases God because ★ families are important to God.**

LIFE APPLICATION

Pick a Fight

Write the following phrases on separate slips of paper:
◆ Whose turn it is to do the dishes
◆ Doing homework before watching TV
◆ Whether to watch a baseball game or a Disney movie
◆ Whether to eat at McDonald's or Pizza Hut
◆ Who gets to ride in the front seat
◆ Who hogs the telephone
◆ Borrowing someone's clothes without asking
◆ Who's always the last one ready to go to school or church

Have everyone re-form their family groups from the Attention Grabber. Give each family one slip of paper.

Say: **You have two minutes to prepare a family feud about what's written on your slip of paper. There are two rules. First, please don't use any bad language. Second, everyone in your family must be involved in your skit.**

After two minutes, call on families to give their skits. Give each group a hearty round of applause.

After all the groups have performed, say: **In your groups, read aloud Ephesians 4:29–5:1. Then, following the advice of those verses, plan a new ending to your skit.**

Allow about a minute for planning; then have groups perform once again.

Say: ★ **Families are important to God. That's why it's important to work together to solve problems, to show that you love each other, and to be ready to forgive.**

Teacher Tip

If you have adults in your class, encourage them to take the roles of children in the skits. The role reversal can be quite entertaining!

Teacher Tip

If you're running short of time, you may want to have family groups simply tell how their problems could be resolved rather than performing again.

COMMITMENT

Funtastic Families

Distribute photocopies of the "Funtastic Families" handout and markers. Have everyone draw or write about their real families in the center of the handout. Then let them share with their family groups what they wrote or drew.

Say: **Now read through the funtastic-family ideas together and tell your family group members which idea you plan to do this week with your family at home.**

CLOSING

Family Affirmations

As everyone is sharing, pass out star stickers.

Say: **Now take a moment to put a star sticker on each member of your family group. As you put the sticker on, say, "You're a funtastic family member because...," and finish the sentence with something nice you've noticed about that person.**

As family groups finish their affirmations, gather everyone in a large circle for a group hug.

Pray: **Lord, thank you for all the different kinds of families we represent. I pray that you'll bless each family and help us all to show your love at home. In Jesus' name, amen.**

Draw or write about your family in the center of the page. Then follow this path to become a funtastic family. Put a star beside each idea you try.

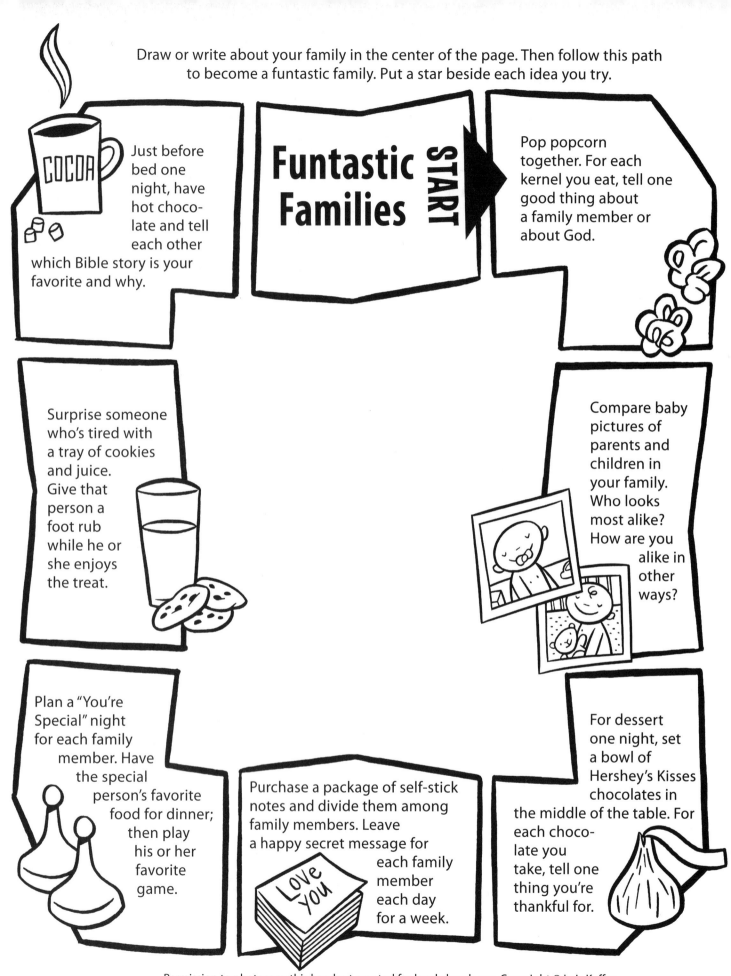

Funtastic Families START

Just before bed one night, have hot chocolate and tell each other which Bible story is your favorite and why.

Pop popcorn together. For each kernel you eat, tell one good thing about a family member or about God.

Surprise someone who's tired with a tray of cookies and juice. Give that person a foot rub while he or she enjoys the treat.

Compare baby pictures of parents and children in your family. Who looks most alike? How are you alike in other ways?

Plan a "You're Special" night for each family member. Have the special person's favorite food for dinner; then play his or her favorite game.

Purchase a package of self-stick notes and divide them among family members. Leave a happy secret message for each family member each day for a week.

For dessert one night, set a bowl of Hershey's Kisses chocolates in the middle of the table. For each chocolate you take, tell one thing you're thankful for.

LESSON AIM

To help kids believe that ★ God will help us through hard times.

OBJECTIVES

Kids will

✓ experience receiving a prize that isn't what they had hoped for,
✓ act out Joseph's story of troubles and triumph,
✓ describe responses to tough situations, and
✓ commit to trusting God when they face tough times.

YOU'LL NEED

❑ 5 containers of different sizes
❑ a plastic tablecloth
❑ masking tape
❑ marshmallows*
❑ photocopies of the "Hard Times" handout (p. 106)
❑ pencils or markers
*Always check for allergies before serving snacks.

BIBLE BASICS

Genesis 39–45

It's impossible to read the story of Joseph without marveling at how he handled the incredible ups and downs of his life. Favorite son to slave. Favored servant to prisoner. Prisoner to second in command of all Egypt. Whew! Most amazing of all is Joseph's steady, level-headed dedication to serving God by doing his best in every circumstance.

In our culture we've come to believe that life owes us a steady job with good retirement income, a comfortable home, more than we need to eat, and regular opportunities for

rest and recreation. If illness, loss of a job, or other financial setbacks come our way, we tend to think that God owes us an explanation.

Joseph might smile at us and shake his head. He didn't find his security in his family or his job. Joseph was content to place his life in the hands of the living God who was as much present in a dark prison as in Pharaoh's palace.

In his adult years, Joseph stands out as one of the Bible's few sterling characters. There's no moral slip, no greed, no glaring faults—just a man who trusted God completely.

Psalm 37:3a, 5

"Trust the Lord and do good" is the Christian's response to every situation in life, good or bad, deserved or undeserved. We can trust God to bring us through—no matter how defeating the circumstances may seem.

UNDERSTANDING YOUR KIDS

Few kids in Western societies realize how much their lifestyles contrast with those of people in less-privileged countries. But affluence doesn't necessarily result in contentment. No matter what their ages are, kids focus on the next gadget they plan to acquire rather than on the bounty they already enjoy.

Kids can learn a lot from the story of Joseph. He shifted from the ranks of the haves to those of the have-nots on a regular basis. Yet we don't hear a whisper of complaint. He always did his best, even when he was treated unfairly. Because he was so focused on God, Joseph could take the best and worst life had to offer.

Use this lesson to challenge kids to look for God's hand in every situation and to rely on God's strength when the going gets tough.

ATTENTION GRABBER

No Fair!

Set up a marshmallow-toss using five containers set in a line, the smallest container in front and the largest in back. Any containers will do. You might start with a #2 tin can and end with a bucket, adding three other containers of increasingly large sizes in between. Spread a plastic tablecloth under the containers so kids will be able to eat the marshmallows that bounce on the floor.

Place one masking tape line on the floor two feet from the first container and a second line three feet from the first container. Younger kids will toss from the closer line, and older kids from the farther.

As kids arrive, give them each five marshmallows.

Say: **I have great prizes for kids who can toss their marshmallows into all five containers.**

Have each child try to toss a marshmallow in each container. After kids have each had their turn, let them retrieve their marshmallows from the containers or from the floor, but don't allow them to eat their marshmallows yet.

After everyone has played, congratulate the kids who got all or most of their marshmallows in the containers.

Then say: **I promised great prizes for getting all your marshmallows in the containers. Here's your prize: You get to eat your marshmallows. By the way, everyone else can eat their marshmallows, too.**

When kids protest, ask:

♦ **What's wrong?** (This isn't fair; you promised us a great prize, but kids who didn't win got the same thing we did.)

Say: **Hmm. This isn't what you expected, is it? But, you see, when I promised you a prize, I never said that the other kids wouldn't get a prize, too.**

Ask:

♦ **Do you still think it's unfair? Why or why not?** (Yes, because I think we should get a better prize; no, because this way everyone gets a treat.)

Say: **Sometimes life surprises us in ways we think are unfair. For instance, you might study hard for a test but get a poor grade. You might get blamed for something you didn't do. Or someone you trust might fail to keep a promise. It seems unfair, but there's not a whole lot you can do about it. The good news is that ★ God will help us through tough times.**

THE FAVORITE SON

(from Genesis 37; 39; 41-45)

Fathers, brothers, sisters, mothers.
Me, my cat, my dog, and others.
Grandmas, uncles, aunts, and cousins.
Family members by the dozens.
How many people live with you?
Eleven or 12, or one or two?

Joseph lived with many others.
Joseph had 11 brothers!
(Count on fingers as you name the brothers.)
Brothers Levi, Asher, Dan,
Judah, Gad, and Simeon.
Reuben, Issachar, Benjamin.
Naphtali and Zebulun.
But Joseph was the favorite son—
his father Jacob's #1.
(Hold up one finger.)

Jacob gave his son a coat.
A brand new coat—then he could gloat.
(Pretend to hold up a coat.)
Joseph had more than the others—
there were no coats for his brothers.
Joseph's coat was the only one,
for Joseph was the favorite son.
(Hug yourself.)

That special coat was quite a sight!
(Make glasses with your fingers.)
Colorful and very bright.
Purple, yellow, pink, and green—
the prettiest coat you've ever seen.
Joseph's coat fit perfectly!
It's beautiful, don't you agree?

The other brothers made a fuss.
(Put hands on hips.)
"Why does he get more than us?"
They began to grumble and pout.
(Make a sour face.)
"Why did father leave us out?"
Tell me now what you would do
if there'd been no gift for you.

One night Joseph had a dream—
his brothers all bowed down to him!
(Bow down.)
The older boys had had enough,
so they decided to get rough.
(Hold up fists.)
"This favorite son has got to go!
Then maybe Dad will love us, too."

The boys threw Joseph in a well.
(Look down.)
Then decided they would tell
old Jacob that his son had died.
That would fix young Joseph's pride!
Then a caravan came by.
The boys said, "Hey—why don't we try
to sell our brother for some money?
Joseph a slave! Isn't that funny?"
(Hold your stomach and laugh.)

His brothers got him in a mess,
but Joseph chose to try his best.
And all along he thought, "You'll see
(point upward)—
the Lord, my God, will set me free."

Even when Joseph was a slave,
he was kind and smart and brave.
Then someone nasty told a tale,
and Joseph ended up in jail!
(Wrap hands around imaginary bars.)
But still he didn't
moan or pout—
he trusted God to work things out.

One day Joseph got a call
to see King Pharaoh in his hall.
(Make a crown with your hands.)
The king was troubled by his dreams.
(Frown.)
He said, "Please tell me what this means."
Joseph helped him understand
that God in heaven had a plan.

"For seven years you'll have good crops
(thumbs up),
but after that, the growing stops.
(Thumbs down.)
Get someone to make a plan
to save up all the food you can."
The king said, "Joseph, you're my man!
(Point.)
I'll make you second in command."

Now that Joseph was in charge,
he built new barns that were quite large.
(Spread arms.)
He gathered food from everywhere
so there would be enough to share.
Then when the ground grew hard and dry,
people came to him to buy.
(Hold out a hand.)

Joseph's brothers came one day.
They traveled there from far away
to get some food for their empty bowls
(cup empty hands)
and stop their stomachs' hungry growls.
(Rub stomach.)

As they bowed before their brother
(bow down),
they mistook him for another.
They didn't see him as the one
who'd been their father's favorite son.
So Joseph tested them to find
(rub your chin)
if their hearts were mean or kind.

Joseph's brothers passed the test.
He knew they wanted what was best.
Joseph hugged them, one by one
(give hugs),
and then before the day was done,
he filled their baskets with good food.
(Circle arms like a basket.)
More and more—they overflowed!

When Joseph's brothers went to pack
(wave goodbye),
they promised to bring their father back.
The family moved to Egypt, where
they lived their lives in Joseph's care.
Then their days were filled with laughter,
and they lived happily ever after.
(Fold arms and nod.)

BIBLE STUDY

Teacher Tip

Rehearse the ballad several times before class so you can do the motions along with the story. Or, choose an older student to tell the story with you. The student can lead the motions as you read the ballad.

If you taught lesson 10 last week, say: **Last week we learned how Joseph's brothers sold him as a slave. Today we're going to review that story, then see what happened to Joseph next.**

Troubles and Triumph (Genesis 37; 39; 41–45)

Say: **Today's Bible story is about a young man who had one tough time after another, and none of it was really his fault. I'll tell the story as a ballad. Watch me carefully and do exactly what I do.**

Read "The Favorite Son," and do the motions in parentheses.

Give a round of applause for kids' participation in the story. Then ask:

♦ **What happened to Joseph that was especially hard or unfair?** (He was sold as a slave; he was put in prison for something he didn't do.)

♦ **Suppose you were put in prison even though you'd never committed a crime. What would you do?** (I'd be angry; I'd try to break out.)

♦ **What special things did Joseph do?** (He still did his best, even though bad things happened to him; he forgave his brothers even though they'd been really mean to him; he saved up enough food for everyone.)

♦ **Why do you think Joseph could do all these good things even when bad things kept happening to him?** (He trusted God; he knew God would work things out.)

Say: ★ **God will help us through hard times. Joseph knew that. Because Joseph trusted God, he kept doing his best in every situation. And that's not always easy to do. Let's explore ways we can follow Joseph's example today.**

LIFE APPLICATION

Teacher Tip

Explain that readers and reporters don't necessarily have to be older kids. Encourage groups to give responsibility to younger kids as well.

Hard Times

Distribute photocopies of the "Hard Times" handout.

Help kids form three groups. Assign each group one of the articles on the handout. Have a volunteer read aloud the verse at the top of the handout.

Then say: **This verse could be Joseph's motto! Joseph was always willing to trust God and do good.**

In just a moment, I'll have you read through your article together and decide how the people in your story could trust God and do good, just as Joseph did.

Explain that each group will need a reader to read the article aloud, a reporter to share the group's discussion with the rest of the class, and several encouragers to make sure everyone gets involved in the discussion.

Call time after about three minutes. Have the reporters tell how their groups decided the people in their stories could trust God and do good.

After each report, open the discussion to the rest of the class and encourage the whole class to brainstorm other ways to trust God and do good in that situation.

COMMITMENT

My Times

Say: **The God who took care of Joseph during all his ups and downs is the same God who takes care of us today. ★ God will help us through hard times, just as he helped Joseph.**

Distribute pencils or markers. Help kids find partners. Make it a point to match older kids with younger partners, and shy kids with outgoing partners.

Say: **There's a blank space on your Hard Times newspaper where you can write or draw your own story. You can tell about a tough situation you faced in the past, one that you're facing right now, or a tough situation you may face in the future. I'll give you about three minutes to write or draw. Then I'll call time and ask you to share your story with your partner.**

After three minutes, call time and have kids share their stories with their partners.

Then say: **Now tell your partner how you could trust God and do good in this situation.**

After partners have shared, bring everyone together. Invite volunteers to tell about their partners' situations and how they could trust God in the midst of them.

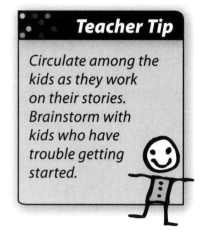

Teacher Tip

Circulate among the kids as they work on their stories. Brainstorm with kids who have trouble getting started.

CLOSING

Trust Pileup

Have kids form a circle, place their handouts on the floor behind them, and link arms.

Say: **Because Joseph trusted God and did his best, thousands and thousands of lives were saved during the great famine. Joseph was just one person. If all of us promise to trust God and do good, think of the good things that could happen. ★ God will help us through hard times. Let's celebrate that by making a pile of hands. When you add your hand to the pile, say, "Trust God and do good!"**

When all the hands are on the pile, pray: **Dear Lord, thank you for the way you helped Joseph through hard times. Help us to trust you and do good, just as Joseph did. Amen.**

HARD TIMES

Anytown, America

"Trust the Lord and do good. Depend on the Lord; trust him, and he will take care of you" (Psalm 37:3a, 5, NIV).

GIRL ACCUSED OF CHEATING

Miss Wompet made Greta Goodgrade stay after school today and miss soccer practice. "Miss Wompet thought I was cheating," Greta reported, "but I wasn't. The person behind me asked how much more time we had to finish our test. I said we had five minutes, but I didn't tell any answers. Now I won't be able to play in this weekend's soccer game because I have to miss today's practice."

FLU CANCELS CAMP PLANS

Several kids from Neighborhood Church had to cancel plans to attend camp when they came down with the flu earlier this week. The group had worked hard to earn money for camp. They had held a carwash, a bake sale, and an auction. "With many of the kids already sick and others exposed to the flu, we decided to cancel camp plans entirely," Pastor Will U. Begood reported.

FLOOD WASHES OUT HOMES

Several area homes were damaged in flash floods over the weekend. "The river just couldn't handle all the rain," said Hi N. Dry, a local builder. "It'll be weeks before things are back to normal." The Red Cross has set up temporary shelters for the flood victims in local churches. "I just want to go home," said one 8-year-old at the Red Cross shelter. "I was supposed to have my birthday party tomorrow."

ADD YOUR STORY HERE

LESSON AIM

To help kids understand that ★ we celebrate God's goodness.

OBJECTIVES

Kids or families will

✓ decorate baskets and make harvest treats to serve in them,

✓ learn about harvest in Bible times,

✓ complete a paper quilt block and offer thanks for God's blessings, and

✓ share the joy of harvest time with others.

Teacher Tip

This lesson works well with an intergenerational class. You may wish to invite families to join you for this session.

YOU'LL NEED

❏ a popcorn popper
❏ a small microwave oven
❏ popcorn*   ❏ cinnamon*
❏ sugar*   ❏ salt*   ❏ butter*
❏ measuring cups and spoons
❏ large bowls and pans
❏ mixing spoons
❏ photocopies of the cinnamon popcorn recipe (p. 112)
❏ medium or large paper grocery bags
❏ curling ribbon or crepe paper streamers
❏ a large, round basket or tray
❏ a stalk of wheat, a jar of flour, and a loaf of bread (optional)
❏ balloons
❏ photocopies of the "Patchwork of Thanks" handout (p. 117)
❏ crayons or markers
❏ scissors
❏ tape
❏ a hole punch
*Always check for allergies before serving snacks.

all-in-one
SUNDAY
SCHOOL

BIBLE BASIS

Deuteronomy 8:1-18

For the people of Israel, harvest time meant days of intense work that culminated the growing season. The threats and hazards were many. Excessive rain or hail could ruin maturing crops. At various times in Israel's history, stronger neighbors swooped down and ruined or stole crops just as they were ready to be harvested. Crops were susceptible to various diseases, drought, and hot winds. Occasionally ravenous swarms of grasshoppers stripped fields clean. Given all these variables, a harvest safely accomplished was truly a sign of God's continued blessing.

The climate and soil of Israel typically allowed for three harvests. Wheat was planted in the fall and harvested in the spring. The Feast of Weeks celebrated the end of the wheat harvest, 50 days after Passover. Grape harvest began in summer and culminated in the Feast of Tabernacles in the fall. In the late summer and fall, as the grape harvest neared its end, dates, figs, and olives ripened.

God clearly meant for his people to celebrate at harvest time. Scripture speaks of it repeatedly: "This festival will be a happy time of celebrating with your sons and daughters, your male and female servants, and the Levites, foreigners, orphans, and widows from your towns. For seven days you must celebrate this festival to honor the Lord your God at the place he chooses, for it is he who blesses you with bountiful harvests and gives you success in all your work. This festival will be a time of great joy for all" (Deuteronomy 16:14-15). The joy mandated here is not based on the abundance of food, but in God's continued blessing on the land and its inhabitants. The people were to remember that when they were slaves in Egypt, God promised to bring them to a land flowing with milk and honey. Each harvest brought a reminder of that promise and of God's faithfulness.

Deuteronomy 26:1-2

God wants us to acknowledge and give thanks for the continuous stream of blessings he pours into our lives. Though our "first fruits" may not be agricultural in nature, we can still honor God with offerings and praises for the abundance we enjoy.

UNDERSTANDING YOUR KIDS

Thanksgiving is a terrific time for kids to focus on God. They aren't distracted by the anticipation of getting things. There are no Thanksgiving stockings or harvest bunnies that bring baskets of goodies. They don't make Thanksgiving lists, nor do they look for presents under a Thanksgiving tree. Somehow this joyful season has not been secularized and commercialized with expectations much beyond turkey and pumpkin pie. How refreshing!

Use this lesson to help kids see that God brings many kinds of blessings into our lives and that it pleases God when we celebrate his goodness.

The Lesson ☺

ATTENTION GRABBER

Cinnamon Harvest

If it's possible, set up a popcorn popper and a small microwave oven in your classroom for this lesson. If your situation doesn't allow that, plan to take kids to a kitchen.

Set up two work centers.

At a cinnamon popcorn center, set out the popcorn popper and microwave, sugar, cinnamon, salt, butter, glass measuring cups and teaspoon measures. You'll also need large bowls or pans, mixing spoons, and photocopies of the cinnamon popcorn recipe.

Set up a basket decorators center with paper grocery bags, a hole punch, scissors, and curling ribbon or crepe paper in harvest colors.

Say: **It's harvest time, and we're here to celebrate! I need cinnamon popcorn makers and basket decorators. The cinnamon popcorn makers will follow the recipe I've set out and use these ingredients to make yummy cinnamon popcorn to share. The basket decorators will use grocery bags and ribbons to make cool-looking baskets that we'll put the popcorn in when we take it to share with others.**

Put an adult, a teenage helper, or a reliable older child in charge of the cinnamon popcorn center. Explain exactly what setting of the microwave to use to melt the butter. (It must be a very low setting.) Emphasize that only kids who handle the ingredients carefully will be allowed to work in the cinnamon popcorn center. Plan to allow kids to make two or three batches so you'll have plenty of cinnamon popcorn to share later in the lesson.

Invite everyone to watch as you make one harvest basket at the basket decorators center. Cut off the top half of a grocery bag; then carefully fold the top down two inches to form a cuff. Pinch and crumple the top slightly to fold the cuff over once more; then smooth it out. Punch a hole through the cuff in the middle of each narrow side. Cut six 30-inch lengths of curling ribbon. Fold three lengths in half, push the loop at the middle through one of the holes in the bag starting from the inside; then pull the ends through the loop and tighten. Repeat on the other side of the bag. Or cut six 2-foot lengths of crepe paper. Twist three ends together, push them through a hole, knot them, and pull the knot tight against the hole. Repeat on the other side of the bag.

Let kids choose the center where they'd like to work. Have

Teacher Tip

If you don't have access to a microwave oven, bring the melted butter to class in covered glass jars. Kids can mix the rest of the ingredients right in the jars. You'll need to bring kitchen towels to wrap around the warm jars so kids can handle them safely.

plenty of bags and ribbon on hand so everyone who wishes to can make a harvest basket. If families are attending this class, encourage each family to make a harvest basket.

Allow everyone to take very small samples of the cinnamon popcorn as it's made. Allow about 10 minutes for kids to work at the centers. Give a two-minute warning before you ask them to begin to clean up. Have kids set the baskets and cinnamon popcorn aside.

Say: ★ **We celebrate God's goodness at harvest time, and our celebration has just begun. Let's find out more about the wonderful feasts and celebrations God planned for his people at harvest time.**

BIBLE STUDY

A Bible-Time Harvest (Deuteronomy 8:1-18)

Say: **Did you know that God actually instructed his people to throw a party at harvest time? That's right. God wanted his people to bring their offerings, give thanks, and have a wonderful time rejoicing and feasting together. Let's read what the Bible says about that.**

Have a volunteer look up and read aloud Deuteronomy 16:13-15 in a kid-friendly Bible.

Say: **God instructed his people to celebrate two harvest feasts—one in the spring, and one in the fall. You see, farmers planted grain in the fall—kind of like our winter wheat. It grew over the winter and ripened after the spring rains. Workers cut the wheat with scythes. A scythe had a sturdy handle and a long, curved blade. I need about four kids to be wheat.** Have four volunteers stand close together. Pretend to swing a scythe near their feet; then have them fall to the ground. Have them remain stiff and straight like a stalk of grain. **Several stalks of grain would fall with one skillful cut. Then another worker would bundle the grain into sheaves.** Roll the children together and pretend to tie them around the middle. **All the sheaves would be gathered onto donkeys or carts and carried to the village threshing floor.** Thank the "wheat children" and have them rejoin the group.

The threshing floor was a big, open space of hard-packed dirt. From the book of Ruth we know that landowners sometimes slept by their piles of grain to protect them from robbers. At the threshing floor, the grain would be spread out. Oxen would be hooked up to a heavy sledge that had

Teacher Tip

To illustrate the steps of the process you've just described, you may want to display a stalk or bundle of wheat, a small jar of whole-wheat flour, and a round loaf of bread or a piece of pita bread.

111

CINNAMON POPCORN

Makes 3 quarts (12 cups) of popcorn.
Pop enough popcorn kernels to measure 12 cups of popcorn.
In a large glass measuring cup, melt ½ cup butter.
Add ¼ cup sugar, ½ teaspoon cinnamon, and ¼ teaspoon salt.
Stir carefully until the sugar is nearly dissolved.
Pour the butter mixture over the popcorn and mix well.
(Optional: Bake in a large pan for 15 minutes at 300 degrees.)

CINNAMON POPCORN

Makes 3 quarts (12 cups) of popcorn.
Pop enough popcorn kernels to measure 12 cups of popcorn.
In a large glass measuring cup, melt ½ cup butter.
Add ¼ cup sugar, ½ teaspoon cinnamon, and ¼ teaspoon salt.
Stir carefully until the sugar is nearly dissolved.
Pour the butter mixture over the popcorn and mix well.
(Optional: Bake in a large pan for 15 minutes at 300 degrees.)

CINNAMON POPCORN

Makes 3 quarts (12 cups) of popcorn.
Pop enough popcorn kernels to measure 12 cups of popcorn.
In a large glass measuring cup, melt ½ cup butter.
Add ¼ cup sugar, ½ teaspoon cinnamon, and ¼ teaspoon salt.
Stir carefully until the sugar is nearly dissolved.
Pour the butter mixture over the popcorn and mix well.
(Optional: Bake in a large pan for 15 minutes at 300 degrees.)

pointed rocks or bits of iron attached to the underside. The oxen would drag the sledge over the grain to separate the heads from the stalks. Sometimes children would get to ride on the sledge to make it heavier.

Once the heads were separated from the stalks, the grain had to be *winnowed.* That meant separating the chaff, the non-edible part, from the good kernels of grain. A harvester would pick up some stalks with a winnowing fork, which was kind of a cross between a pitchfork and a rake. He would toss the stalks into the air, and the heavier heads would fall first while the stalks blew away.

Then the heads of grain would go into a basket. Pour several kernels of popcorn into a large, round basket. Toss the kernels into the air, and catch them again in the basket. When they were tossed in the air, a slight wind would catch the chaff and blow it away, while the good kernels of grain would fall back into the basket. Set the basket aside.

People with small fields might store the grain in clay jars. Wealthy farmers with lots of land stored it in barns. When it was time to make bread, the grain had to be ground into flour. It could be placed in a large stone bowl and ground with a smaller stone. Or it could be milled between two large stones. Then, finally, flour could be made into bread. Whew!

Ask:

♦ Where does your bread come from? (The store; the cupboard.)

Say: Getting a piece of bread may seem like a simple thing to us. But when people in Bible times ate a piece of bread, they remembered plowing the field; planting the seeds; waiting during the long winter months; praying for rain in the spring; praying for good, dry weather for harvest; cutting the grain; bundling it; taking it to the threshing floor; winnowing it; grinding it into flour; and finally baking the bread. And when that process was over, they were ready to celebrate and give thanks!

Those families who were able would go up to Jerusalem to celebrate the grain harvest at the Feast of Weeks. Everyone would take loaves of bread made from the new grain and give thanks at the Temple. Those who couldn't go to Jerusalem would celebrate and give thanks at the synagogues in their own villages.

The second harvest of the year was the grape harvest. That started in the summer and extended into early fall. Most grapes grew on hillsides above the villages, where it was cooler. The vineyards were separate from the other fields and often were far from the owners' houses. As the grapes ripened during the summer, families might move out by their vineyards and sleep there to protect their grapes.

Some grapes were kept for drying and making raisins. The rest were crushed to make wine. And what a celebration that was! Let's blow up some balloons to represent bunches of grapes.

Allow each student to blow up a balloon and tie it off. Have everyone stand in a circle around the balloons. **The grapes were placed in a round, stone vat called a wine press. And villagers stomped on the grapes to squeeze out the juice that ran into another vat below. Let's stomp our grapes!** Lead kids in stomping the balloons until they've all popped. (Then discard all broken balloon pieces promptly to avoid a choking hazard.)

You can imagine that they had a great time, just as we did! There was a lot of singing and dancing. The grape juice was poured into clay jars. And when that was done, the harvest season was complete.

Then everyone gathered offerings for the Lord and prepared for the Feast of Tabernacles. It was kind of like Thanksgiving and New Year's all rolled into one! Every family used branches to make little shelters in the streets and on the rooftops. They lived in these shelters for a week. You can imagine the festive atmosphere in the city with all the visitors bringing their offerings to the Temple, all the little shelters, and lots of good food to share. Merchants brought special things to sell because they knew the visitors would be in the city for just a short time. Uncles and aunts and cousins who rarely saw each other got to spend time together.

But the high point of the whole celebration was bringing offerings to the Temple and thanking God for blessing the year with a good harvest. Even though we can't travel to Jerusalem, we can have our own special harvest celebration right now. Let's find out how ★ we can celebrate God's goodness.

LIFE APPLICATION

Patchwork of Thanks

Have a volunteer find and read aloud Deuteronomy 26:1-2a. Ask:

♦ **Since some of us don't have a harvest of fruit or vegetables, what can we offer thanks for?** (Our homes and cars; our jobs; our good health.)

Say: ★ **We celebrate God's goodness at harvest time, and I have a unique way for us to offer our thanks. Our celebration will involve giving a basket of thanks to God.**

Distribute the crayons or markers, scissors, and the "Patchwork of Thanks" handout. Have participants form groups of four. Place older participants in groups with nonreaders to help the younger ones complete their quilt blocks.

Say: **Cut out your quilt block on the outside heavy lines. Then answer the three questions on the quilt block—you may write or draw your answers. Then share them with your group. When you've finished answering the questions and discussing your answers, fill in the triangles with flowers in one color. Then fill in the basket shape with the squiggles in another color. Use whatever colors you wish. Leave the top square and the two side triangles blank.**

Allow groups about 10 minutes to work on their handouts and discuss what they're drawing and writing. Circulate among the groups to offer help and ideas as needed. Encourage everyone to give thoughtful answers to each question.

Give a two-minute warning before you ask everyone to clean up and put away the scissors and markers or crayons. Then gather everyone in a circle. Have kids place their finished quilt blocks on the floor in front of them. Invite kids to tell about the interesting things various people in their groups gave thanks for.

COMMITMENT

A Wall of Thanks

After several kids have shared, say: **Remember how the Scripture we read earlier talked about bringing an offering in a basket? Now each of you has a basket to offer in thanks to the Lord. ★ We'll celebrate God's goodness as we assemble our baskets into a beautiful patchwork of thanks.**

One by one, have groups tape their quilt blocks to a wall or table. Help them arrange the blocks in a solid cluster to give the impression of a quilt. As you arrange the quilt, have a good singer lead favorite praise songs or play music from a CD.

Gather in front of the complete patchwork of thanks. If you wish, sing some lively songs with a Jewish theme, such as "It Is Good to Give Thanks" or "Jehovah Jireh." Then pray a prayer similar to this one: **Dear Lord, we offer you our thanks for the wonderful blessings represented on this wall. Thank you for giving us a good year. Thank you for the blessings we enjoy each day. Help us to remember that all these good things come from your hand. In Jesus' name we pray, amen.**

Teacher Tip

You might want to take a photograph of the kids standing around the patchwork of thanks. Then have a print made for each child.

CLOSING

Celebrate!

Say: **Now it's time to share our joy with other folks here at church! In just a moment we'll form groups to distribute the cinnamon popcorn we made earlier. As you offer the popcorn, explain that we're celebrating God's goodness. Invite everyone to come and look at our patchwork of thanks and enjoy more cinnamon popcorn.**

Assign kids to groups that will each walk around other parts of your church. Designate one person in each group to carry a harvest basket of cinnamon popcorn. Explain that the other kids can invite everyone to visit the class and see the patchwork of thanks.

When visitors come to class, have kids point out their own quilt blocks and tell about the things they're thankful for. You may wish to leave the quilt on display for another week. If you have kids who won't be back, let them take their quilt blocks. Rearrange the remaining blocks to make a solid quilt.

Give everyone a copy of the cinnamon popcorn recipe to take home. Encourage participants to celebrate God's goodness each time they make it!

PATCHWORK OF THANKS

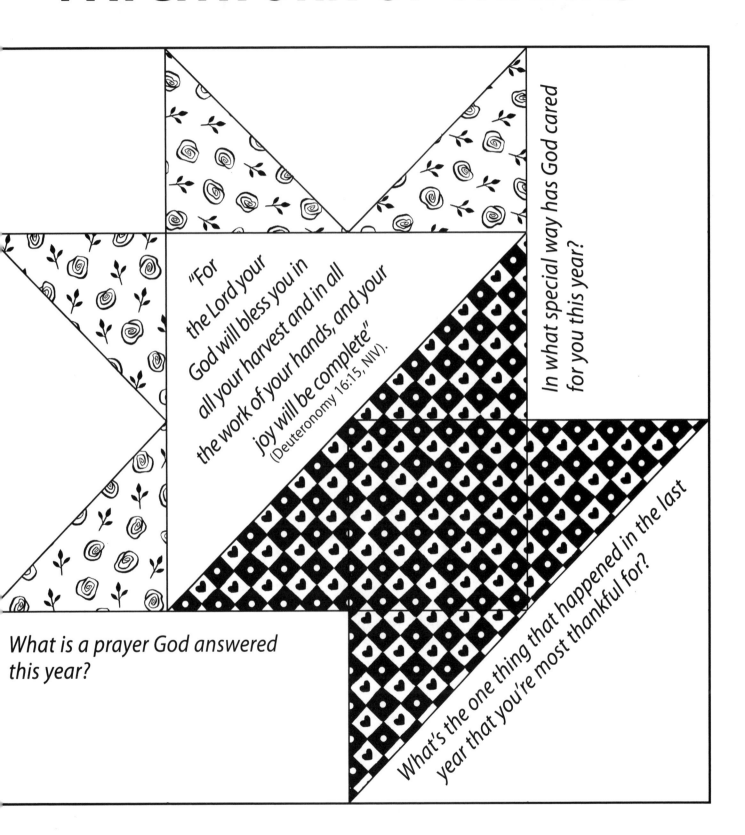

In what special way has God cared for you this year?

"For the Lord your God will bless you in all your harvest and in all the work of your hands, and your joy will be complete" (Deuteronomy 16:15, NIV).

What is a prayer God answered this year?

What's the one thing that happened in the last year that you're most thankful for?

Published in *All-in-One Sunday School Volume 1* by Group Publishing, Inc., 1515 Cascade Ave., Loveland, CO 80538.

LESSON AIM

To help kids discover that ★ because God takes care of us, we can share with others.

OBJECTIVES

Kids will

✓ discover how sharing can benefit everyone,
✓ learn how a woman in the Bible shared the last food she had,
✓ make an inventory of what they have to share, and
✓ identify three things they will share this week.

YOU'LL NEED

❏ a container of peanut butter*
❏ a jar of jelly*
❏ a loaf of bread*
❏ four knives
❏ paper plates
❏ napkins
❏ photocopies of the "Share Sheet" handout (p. 125)
❏ markers
❏ masking tape
❏ Bibles
*Always check for allergies before serving snacks.

BIBLE BASIS

1 Kings 17:1-16

This story is set against a time of great famine in the land of Israel. The prophet Elijah told King Ahab that God would not allow rain or dew until the king repented of his wicked ways. Then Elijah ran for his life!

Elijah eventually made his way to the home of a widow and

all-in-one
SUNDAY
SCHOOL

asked for food. Widows had no rights and few defenders in Bible times. Asking a widow for food would be like asking a homeless person for a blanket. But the woman realized this was no ordinary person who asked. She recognized Elijah's request as God's will and willingly obeyed.

We can find joy in sharing even the things that are most precious to us when our sharing is done in obedience to God's will and in recognition that God, our provider, will not fail us.

Philippians 4:19

This remarkable promise was not written by a wealthy person surrounded by all the comforts of life. It was written by Paul, probably while he was in prison or under house arrest in Rome. Paul's circumstances give special meaning to his faith that God would care for those who care for the needs of others.

UNDERSTANDING YOUR KIDS

"Mine!" is one of the first words toddlers learn to speak. "My" and "me" are quick to follow. Our healthy instincts for self-preservation carry over very naturally into "self-ishness." There are those few, rare children who seem to be naturally bighearted and generous. But most kids learn sharing by example and by receiving praise and attention for generous behavior.

Children share more readily as they get older and become more mature. Some 4- and 5-year-olds may not want to share at all—they may be perfectly happy to take whatever interests them and to go play by themselves in a corner. Most kids are well into their elementary school years before they learn to share for the sheer joy of meeting a need or making another person happy.

all-in-one SUNDAY SCHOOL

The Lesson ☺

ATTENTION GRABBER

The Impossible Sandwich

As kids arrive direct them into four groups.

Say: **We're going to start off today with a treat.**

Give the first group a container of peanut butter, the second group a jar of jelly, the third group a loaf of bread, and the fourth group four plastic knives. Give everyone paper plates and napkins.

Then say: **Go ahead and eat!**

Kids may or may not figure out that they can all enjoy peanut butter and jelly sandwiches if the groups all share what they have. Drop a little hint like, "I wonder what would happen if everyone shared …"

When everyone is finally enjoying peanut butter and jelly sandwiches, ask the kids who received only jelly or knives:

♦ **What was it like at the beginning when you only had a jar of jelly or a few knives?** (I didn't know what to do; I wished we'd gotten the butter; I hoped the people who got the other stuff would share with us.)

Ask the kids who received the bread:

♦ **How did you feel about getting something you could eat right away when other kids didn't?** (I felt lucky; I felt sorry for the other kids; I wanted to share right away.)

♦ **What was it like when everyone started sharing?** (I got excited; I felt a lot better.)

♦ **When is it hard to share things?** (When it seems like I have to do all the giving; when it's something I really want for myself.)

♦ **When is it easy to share?** (When there's plenty to go around; when it doesn't really feel like I'm giving up anything.)

Say: **Today you're going to help me tell a story from the Bible about a woman who shared, even when it was really hard. We'll be learning that ★ because God takes care of us, we can share with others.**

BIBLE STUDY

A Little to Share (1 Kings 17:1-16)

Practice each of these cues and responses with the kids:

♦ When I say "brook," everybody say "babble, babble" and make piano fingers, like water running in a stream.

♦ When I say "ravens," everybody flap your arms with your elbows out and say "caw, caw."

♦ When I say "Elijah," the boys point upward and say "the Tishbite."

Take a moment to explain that Elijah was a famous prophet. He was called Elijah the Tishbite because he came from the town of Tishbeh.

♦ When I say "widow," the girls pull their hands down over their faces like a veil.

♦ When I say "bread," everybody rub your tummies and say "yum, yum."

Then say: **Ready? Here we go with the story "Elijah and the Widow."**

Read aloud "Elijah and the Widow" on page 122. Pause after each underlined word to let kids do their actions.

After the story, ask:

♦ **If she only had a little food left, why did the widow share it?** (Elijah told her God wouldn't let her run out of oil until it rained again and people could grow more food.)

♦ **Why did she believe Elijah?** (She knew he was a prophet from God.)

Say: **The interesting thing about this story is God made sure the widow never ran out of oil and flour. So the bread she shared with Elijah wasn't really her own—it came from God. ★ Because God takes care of us, we can share with others.**

God made a promise to take care of the widow when she shared her bread. God makes a promise like this to us, too, in the book of Philippians.

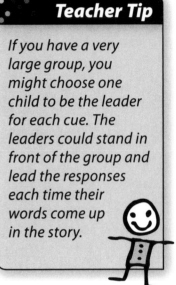

Teacher Tip

If you have a very large group, you might choose one child to be the leader for each cue. The leaders could stand in front of the group and lead the responses each time their words come up in the story.

LIFE APPLICATION

Sharing Time

Give kids each a photocopy of the "Share Sheet" handout, a marker and a piece of masking tape. Have a volunteer read Philippians 4:19 aloud.

Say: **Another famous Bible person, the Apostle Paul, counted on people to share with him. Paul was arrested and put in jail for teaching people about Jesus. His friends in different churches shared food and clothes and money with him. And he told those people who shared with him that**

ELIJAH AND THE WIDOW

Once there was a wicked king named Ahab. He was so wicked, God sent the prophet Elijah to talk to him. "There won't be any rain until you repent of your evil ways," Elijah told the king. This made the wicked King Ahab very angry. So God told Elijah to go hide by a brook. God said, "You can drink from the brook, and I will send ravens with bread for you."

So Elijah went to the brook. Every morning the ravens brought him bread and meat. And even though there was no rain and it was very dry in the whole country, Elijah could drink from the brook.

But finally the brook dried up. So God sent Elijah to the town of Zarephath where he found a kind widow gathering sticks for a fire. "Would you bring me some bread?" Elijah asked the widow. The widow answered, "I don't have any bread, just a little oil and flour, enough to make just one more meal for me and my son."

Elijah said, "Make me some bread first. God will not let you run out of oil and flour until it rains again. The widow did as Elijah said. She made bread for Elijah and herself and her son for many days.

Just as God promised, the oil and flour never ran out. There was always enough to make more bread. God took care of Elijah and the kind widow who shared, and God can take care of you, too!

God would keep on taking care of their needs, just as God took care of the widow who shared with Elijah.

Have someone read aloud Philippians 4:19 again.

Say: **This promise is for us, too, when we share what we have with people in need. The question is: What do we have to share? We're going to find out!**

Have kids find partners. Make sure your youngest students who are just learning to read and write are paired with older students who can help them. If you have more than 20 kids in your class, you may want to do this activity in two groups.

Say: **Write your own name on the blank line at the top of your Share Sheet. Then ask your partner to tape it to your back.**

Explain that each pair will get together with all the other

pairs. Kids will take turns writing on each person's Share Sheet what they think that person has to share with others. Encourage kids to think about everything from hugs and friendly smiles to allowances and video games.

Keep kids moving around the classroom two by two until each set of partners has written on the Share Sheets of all the other pairs.

Say: **Now it's time to see what other people think you have to share! Take off your partner's Share Sheet and hand it to him or her.**

Give kids a moment to look over what people wrote on their Share Sheets. Then ask:

♦ **What's it like to see all the things you have to share?** (It's surprising; it makes me feel good.)

Discuss the fact that everything comes from God in the end. Allowances may come from parents, but parents get their jobs and their abilities to work from God. If we have friendly smiles and hugs to share, it's because God put love for other people in our hearts.

Then say: **Maybe you're thinking of something you have to share that nobody wrote on your Share Sheet. Go ahead and write or draw it now.**

Give kids a moment to think and write or draw. Encourage older kids to help younger ones with ideas.

Say: **Now look over your whole list and decide if each thing on it would be easy or hard for you to share. Put a circle around the things that would be easy for you to share. Underline things that would be hard for you to share. Then tell your partner why you marked things the way you did.**

Allow a couple of minutes for kids to mark their lists and talk with their partners.

Teacher Tip

The job of writing on each other's back is easier if kids use markers, but make sure they are washable markers that won't bleed through the Share Sheets and stain kids' clothes. Crayons work well also.

COMMITMENT

Choosing to Share

After two or three minutes, call time, and say:
Choose three things from your list you'd like to share with someone during the coming week. Draw a box around those things. Then tell your partner what you're going to share and who you're going to share each thing with.

★ **Because God takes care of us, we can share with others.**

CLOSING

Our Sharing God

Bring everyone together and ask for a pair-share, where each person tells one thing his or her partner is going to share this week.

Then say: **The neat thing about sharing things God gives us is that we don't need to worry about running out. He promises in Philippians 4:19 to take care of our needs as we take care of the needs of others.**

Close with prayer, asking God to give kids a generous spirit and to help them follow through on the sharing they've planned for this week.

SHARE SHEET